STRONGER THAN EVER

STRONGER THAN EVER

Empowering Stories From 16 Women Whose Courage Can Inspire Us All

Queens In Business

STRONGER THAN EVER
Empowering Stories From 16 Women Whose Courage Can Inspire Us All

© 2021 Queens In Business

ISBN: 9798843611347 Paperback

Edited By: Sunna Coleman

Cover Designed By: Tanya Grant - The TNG Designs Group Limited

Acknowledgements

By Sunna Coleman
Chief Editor and
Co-Founder of Queens In Business Club

Being an entrepreneur is no easy feat. It takes true courage to put yourself out there, work tirelessly to get your business off the ground, and be brave enough to work on yourself along the way. It can be a struggle from time to time, and that's why it is so important to come to the realisation that you are not alone in this. Surround yourself with a community who understands exactly what you are going through – it really makes a world of difference.

I'd like to say thank you to my fellow Co-Founders, Chloë, Carrie, Shim and Tanya, who give me the courage to keep pushing boundaries in business and go further than I had ever dreamed of.

A special thank you to Angela and Gaby, our talented publishing assistants whose hard work makes this book possible. To Tanya, for her incredible design work on the cover, and to Alex for helping support us with every single challenge we ever throw at her!

And as always, we are thankful for you, the reader, for seeing the value in this book and choosing to surround yourself with inspiring stories that will teach you, encourage you, and remind you of how strong you really are.

Dedication

This book is dedicated to those who have undergone the unthinkable and come out the other side as courageous role models, giving those they inspire the strength to do the same.

With love,
Queens In Business Club

Table Of Contents

Introduction

In order to be in charge of your own destiny, you need to learn how to grow into the bravest version of yourself – the one that blossoms even in the toughest of times. We can falter and fall during difficult moments. Or we can soar and shift into a new direction altogether.

Those who build successful businesses aren't that different from you. Like you, they also have to be constantly courageous, strong, and ready to expect the unexpected especially when the adversities of life befall them.

This work is the compilation of 16 women. An archive that highlights their experiences of awakening during dark times. When the temptation of giving up lured them in, they fought tirelessly to sever the ties to anchors that kept them from rising above. The choice to fathom up the strength to create their own narratives ultimately changed the trajectory of their lives, leading them to build businesses that influence communities.

Feel empowered as you read the words in this book to overcome any difficult experiences you are facing today. Because no matter who you are, we believe that you will discover similarities between your life and the plurality of experiences these 16 women from around the world have faced.

Wearing their vulnerabilities and scars as a badge of honour, the women in this book peel back the layers of their own personal journeys to reveal how they created their soaring empires. May their chorus of voices give you the strength to raise yours. And as you face a new day with a new set of challenges and hardships, may the lessons you learn from their unique experiences make you stronger than ever.

Step Into Your Greatness

Elisa Bisello

Coach, Property Investor, Co-Founder of
SB Relocations Ltd and SB Walls & More Ltd

"When you play it too safe, you're taking the biggest risk of your life." – Barbara Sher

Have you ever felt trapped?

I was born and raised in a city in the North-East part of Italy. Growing up, there was pressure from society to get a degree, get a good job and work hard to move up the ladder. It was the way it had to be to be successful.

My parents have always wanted the best for me. I wasn't pressured by my family to get a degree, but I really felt the pressure from the outside, especially from the work environment.

I studied foreign languages at high school and I got the highest grade. I was such a good student that I qualified for a bursary and I went to London for two months of work experience. It was unpaid at the Italian Tourist Board, my first time away from home for such a long time!

I was thrilled. I enjoyed the experience and it reinforced the love for other countries and cultures that I already had very strong within me. However, this great experience came to an end and it was time to go home. It was the end of August then.

In Italy, to access most university courses, you have to pass a test, but this test takes place in August. As I was in London at that time, the option was either to end my work experience earlier (which would have triggered penalties, lots of paperwork, change of flights, disappointment from the school, etc) or to go for a course that did not require me to pass a test. Although my choice would have been a course accessible through a test, I chose what I felt was the most suitable course for me between the courses that didn't have an admission test.

So I went to university and graduated with top marks, while doing part-time jobs like becoming an artistic gymnastics teacher for kids, waitress in a restaurant, cashier at an ice rink and teaching English to high school students. I was following the path to satisfy what society was expecting from me and with brilliant results. I was nailing it!

After graduating from university, I had to get a good job and I had to find it quickly, then work hard to move up the ladder. This is what I thought to be the path to success. However, the job market at that time wasn't great in Italy. There were a lot of regulations and opportunities for employers to hire people with little investment and commitment. You had to call yourself extremely lucky if you could get a permanent job, even if this was with basic pay.

So I ended up accepting the first role that I was offered. This wasn't a very clear role. The company was small and a high degree of flexibility was required. I ended up doing sales, customer service, debt collection, accounts assistant, stock check, purchasing, physical order preparation, you name it – there's a high chance that I've done it!

I was so proud. I was doing great.

Even though I didn't have a contract and the pay was low (sometimes absent) with really long work hours, I was sure I was on the right path to success and to a fulfilled life. My boss used to tell me that I wouldn't find anything out there paying much more than what I was getting from him (and when I was getting it). Not having any other experience in an office job, I believed him.

The months passed and one day I had to go to the Chamber of Commerce to request a company certificate. While waiting at the counter, my eye fell on a leaflet about an export sales course funded by public funds. Reading the word 'export' brought me back to my work experience in London and resuscitated my strong feelings and appreciation towards other cultures.

Additionally, it was fully funded. I took it as a sign. But here it is, the monkey on my shoulder, telling me that there are only a bunch of places available. "Why on earth would they pick me? Surely there are other people more knowledgeable and more experienced. You are not good enough to make it in the selection." Besides, I had just 48 hours to put together all the documentation needed for the application. "Stay where you are to avoid disappointment," the monkey goes again.

The monkey was very loud, but I decided to play deaf and follow my instinct. I applied and... I was accepted!

After six months I got my diploma and an opportunity for three months of work experience at the Special Agency of the Chamber of Commerce dealing with export markets.

How do I tell my boss now?? Booking a meeting to inform him of my decision was extremely difficult. See, I am a people pleaser and I don't like to be the cause of disappointment and for this reason, I often neglect what I want for myself. Acknowledging this personality trait of mine has been a great achievement because I can now work on it.

Going from a paid job to unpaid work experience was scary. Although the pay wasn't great, at least I was getting something. I knew I had to make the most of it to get the right experience and to then find a good job. It turns out that after three months, the management was so happy that I was offered to stay for an additional six months. This time with an official employment contract with holidays and lunch allowance, although it was a temporary position.

My contract was then renewed for another year and eventually I was given a permanent position. Now we are talking! I finally had a good and permanent job, in a reliable company, with a guaranteed salary at the end of the month.

Leaving The Certain For The Uncertain

After his graduation, my boyfriend decided to move to the UK to improve his English. What I initially thought would be a temporary experience abroad to improve his language skills turned out to be a one way ticket to the UK. To be fair, he kept telling me that he didn't want to stay in Italy, but I just didn't want to hear. Afterall, I had finally secured myself a good job, I couldn't possibly risk losing it.

The separation wasn't easy. We had been living together for four years before his move to the UK. I could hear him saying that he wasn't thinking of coming back and asking me to go with him, but I kept telling myself that his trip was just temporary and he would come back at some point, so I just had to hold the fort for some time while he was away.

The way our brain works is incredible. It is trained to keep us safe and this is exactly what my brain was doing with me: trying to keep me safe. I had worked very hard to create what I thought was the ideal life for me and now that I had achieved all the goals society expected me to achieve, I couldn't throw everything in the bin and start afresh. Too risky.

The weeks went by, then the months. The hope of seeing my boyfriend coming back was decreasing day by day. He was happy there and he kept asking me to go and join him.

Meanwhile, on my side I started feeling miserable. I wasn't fulfilled. Despite me working so hard, there was no chance to climb the career ladder in this place. But it was a full-time job, such an achievement at that time. All my life I'd convinced myself that this is what a perfect life should be. Up until then, I didn't have any other experiences, so I didn't know anything different. I had created myself a nice and warm comfort zone that was making me feel safe, although unhappy.

My discontent was getting stronger and it made me start questioning my current situation. I started wondering if it was time for a change, if leaving what I had behind me to start afresh was actually what was needed for me to be happy again. But the more I was talking to friends and colleagues, the more I was hearing, "Don't do it. Don't leave the old road for the new one. It is risky. Think about what can happen if it goes wrong. You've got a permanent role now, are you crazy to leave? I have friends who went to the UK and came back shortly after because they could not find a job and ended up broke."

Only now I realise that I was surrounded by negative and risk averse people. I could hear them, but inside me, I was feeling like a butterfly in a glass bell. I couldn't help but wonder, what if it goes right?

Finally, I decided to follow my instinct once again. I knew what I needed to do. Resignation letter in one hand and a one way ticket to the UK in the other. I was ready to join my boyfriend and start a new chapter.

The Big Change

When moving to the UK, I didn't have any particular expectations apart from getting a good job (of course) and hoping that I had made the right choice, but what happened exceeded everything I could have possibly imagined. After two weeks from landing in the UK, I was offered a job as export sales support (maternity cover) in a beauty company. This then became a permanent position and I got two promotions in two years. All this without them even asking for my degree!

After 12 months exactly, my boyfriend and I were holding the keys to our first home. The following year we got married and shortly after, we purchased our first investment property in the UK.

I learnt that our fears and limiting beliefs can determine our actions. If we are brave enough to be open minded and push ourselves out of our comfort zone, great things can happen.

Then came 2020 – a very peculiar year for the whole world. When the pandemic hit, unanticipated changes had to be made in daily life; suddenly, the whole world shut down. What initially seemed to be nice for a change (working from home and avoiding a two and a half hour commute every day) resulted in something unexpected.

Being in lockdown was a challenging period for many people, but for a 'people person' like me, having to stay at home and not have in-person interactions was particularly tough. All of a sudden no more contact, no more hugs, interactions only through a screen. It felt so cold and detached from reality. A lot of people lost their jobs during this time, but my husband and I were among the lucky ones to still have one. It took a while to adapt to the new situation, but I thought that once I adapted everything would be fine.

The days were going by and we were finding ourselves working longer and longer hours. Even though we were spending 24 hours a day under the same roof, we were barely seeing each other. We were starting our working day early in the morning and finishing late in the afternoon, even in the evening at times. We were so tired that we were grabbing a quick bite for dinner, sometimes not even having the energy to chat about our day, and we were going straight to bed. My initial hopes of having more free time due to working from home ended up being unrealistic. We were tired and stressed and not having any 'us time' anymore.

We had been trying to start a family for a while, but we hadn't been successful. I have HPV (human papillomavirus) and I have had to have yearly check-ups due to the presence of abnormal cells in my cervix (these are precancerous cells). When the lockdown was announced, absolute priority was given to people affected by Covid-19 and all routine health visits were put on hold.

I was due for my yearly check up at the end of March, but this was cancelled. I was told that it was highly recommended to wait for my visit to be done before trying for a family, just in case the situation with my cervix had gotten worse and I needed an operation. The stress and frustration of having to stop trying was now adding to the fact that I was getting negative tests. Every... single... month.

When I was finally given the green light to start trying again, I was stressed out because I had 'lost' precious time. I thought that my biological clock was ticking and I needed to hurry. At the same time, I kept being very busy at work and being the committed person that I am, I was prioritising my job over my wellbeing.

As women, we are biologically born to give life and nurture it. Consequently, caring for others is in our nature and we can end up neglecting ourselves and our needs to be able to help and support others. For the following few months, I had to keep dealing with the frustration of more and more negative tests, while my friends were announcing that they were expecting. It was just becoming too much.

But then one day, to my great surprise the second pink line appeared. I can still feel goosebumps while writing this story. There is nothing better than receiving good news after having desired something so badly. We were over the moon, we were finally becoming a family of three. I announced it to my husband and we hugged and cried happy tears. I really wanted to shout it to the world.

Life kept being hectic and I kept working long hours and prioritising work over myself. Until one day, I started to feel acute cramps in my abdomen. I wanted to keep calm but it was very difficult. I was in pain and I was scared. We went to A&E, where we were delivered the news: we lost our baby.

Putting Myself First
If there is one positive thing about touching the bottom, it is that from there we can only rise.

When I found out that I had lost my baby, I was devastated and I could not stop crying. I was heartbroken. But then I decided to step out of the situation and look at it from a different perspective.

I am a strong believer that things happen for us, not to us. This mindset shift allows me to be positive and solution-oriented, rather than living with a 'why me?' mindset. There wasn't much I could do about the baby, and to keep feeling sad about it wouldn't have helped. Instead, I could take action and make a change.

My body was clearly telling me that I needed to make changes to my lifestyle. It is then that I realised the importance of not underestimating these signs. So armed with courage, I decided to start prioritising myself and saying those dreadful "nos" that for a people pleaser are so difficult to say. No more long hours; no more skipping lunch breaks or waiting until the very last minute to have a toilet break; no more stressing about work. I was determined to say "yes" to myself for a change, even though this could be a not-so-popular decision in the corporate environment.

Never underestimate the power of looking after yourself. My choices had such an impact on me, so much so that ten months later we were welcoming our gorgeous baby Lorenzo to this world and I tested negative for HPV for the first time after seven years.

Why Fit In When You Were Born To Stand Out?
"There's no easy way to tell you this, Elisa, but I am afraid your role is at high risk of redundancy."

These words still resonate in my head, clear as a lightning bolt. Redundancies happen, things change. But when you are still getting used to your new life as a mum and going through the changes and challenges that come with your new 'role', being told that you don't have a job to go back to when you are seven months into your maternity leave can be tough to accept.

I don't hide that this came as a shock initially. I felt lost. All my commitment, my hard work, my early and my late hours, sometimes even weekends, dedicated to the company did not stop this from happening.

I had been working in the corporate world for most of my life before expecting my baby and I've always been the model employee, the dedicated and loyal person and hard worker that would always go the extra mile to meet the company's interests and requests, even though this was to the detriment of my personal life and my wellbeing.

In fact, one of the reasons I have always struggled to hand in my resignation is because I didn't want to cause any trouble for the company I was working for when leaving. When I found out that I was expecting, I announced it in the early days, because I wanted to give them plenty of time to plan for my replacement. In my last month before my maternity leave, I invested a lot of time preparing a very detailed handover and during my maternity leave, I went to visit the office to update my team on my plans for my return. This was so they could plan accordingly. I thought I had everything covered, but it turns out that my employer had other plans.

"There are some other vacant positions in the company, you can check them out and apply for them if you wish."

No roles were appealing to me, but initially I was tempted to just apply for one. Here it was again, the monkey on my shoulder telling me to go for it because it would be too risky to be unemployed. It was fogging my free thinking.

Our comfort zone is like a cosy blanket that we instinctively turn to during uncertain times. It is a bubble we nicely fit into but it also limits ourselves to what we already know. Stepping out of our comfort zone is scary because we leave the certain for the uncertain. But guess what, this is exactly what makes us grow.

Instead, I decided that this was the time to follow my entrepreneurial path and my new-found passion for coaching. I knew that moving from the beauty industry to property and coaching was a total career change. Going from a regular monthly paycheck to no paycheck at all would have put a lot of pressure on our family. Running three businesses with a little one to look after would have been a big challenge. But I was determined to make it work.

Believe And You Can Achieve

Life in lockdown was difficult and stressful. I realised that this was not the way I wanted to live my life and that I needed to make a change if I wanted to have more freedom and more time.

It is then, that with my husband, we started to think about having our own business. If we had to work so hard, then why not do it for ourselves?

Property was something that I knew was worth exploring. We already had two investment properties and we knew that this could be a good way to get passive income, which is key to getting time freedom. But the fear of debt was blocking me. Additionally, there was a lot of work on my mindset that had to be done.

"I have never had a business before, I don't know where to start, I don't know how to be an entrepreneur, I don't think I have the skills, it is risky."

Does that sound familiar?

It is then that I decided to start investing in professional training and mentorship. Having been a model student in the past, I knew that studying the property strategies was the easy part. I recognised that the biggest challenge was to shift my belief system and to go from, "I can't do this because I'm not good enough" to "I can certainly do this because I am good enough". You have probably heard the phrase: "If you think you can or you can't, you are probably right". I needed to work on my self-confidence.

So I invested in myself and came across some brilliant mentors.

Working on my mindset has had a huge impact on me, both as an entrepreneur and a person. I no longer fear debt because I now know the difference between good debt and bad debt. I believe that I have what it takes to be a successful entrepreneur - not only did I co-found and grow two property businesses while expecting a baby and working full-time, but I'm now in the process of starting my coaching business. I know for certain that I don't need a good job to be successful because the definition of success is personal to each individual and not determined by others.

It is my belief that when you keep an open mind and invest in yourself, opportunities knock on your door. I kept working with my mentors to improve my speaking skills and property knowledge. The cherry on the cake was joining the Queens In Business Club in December 2021. I remember being at Reign Like A Queen – their end of year event – and being in awe of these amazing female entrepreneurs. When the opportunity to join the club presented itself, I didn't think twice and signed up. Little did I know that just two months in, they would let me take on the role of a Director at the club.

This happened thanks to my amazing husband who believes and encourages me, to the incredible Queens In Business Club Co-Founders for the opportunity, but ultimately, because I had the courage of believing in myself and stepping up.

If there is one thing that I would tell my younger self, it is to not let anyone make her believe that she is not good enough. To keep believing in herself and to always have the courage to do what is best for herself, even though it is not what society thinks or requires.

Embrace change. The comfort zone is there to make us feel safe, but it is when you stretch yourself and you put yourself in an uncomfortable – maybe scary – situation that growth happens. Be comfortable with the uncomfortable.

As we are approaching the end of this chapter, I would like to celebrate you for reading this book. By doing this, you are giving yourself permission to get inspired by the stories of other Queens just like you. By getting this book, you chose to do something for yourself, and this, I strongly believe, is an act of courage.

Regardless of where you are right now in your entrepreneurial journey, remember that you've got this and that you don't have to do this journey alone. Find yourself a community of like-minded people who can guide, help and support you along the way. I hope that you have been inspired to take action and remember, it is never too late to change, but change must come from within you.

One day or day one: you decide.

About Me

I am an award winning property investor, international speaker, coach, loving wife and proud mum.

At the age of twenty-seven I left my job, family, friends and settled life in Italy to start a new chapter in a new country.

After spending over 10 years in the corporate world and experiencing burnout , Covid-19 made me realise that time is precious, that there is more to life than a good job and a career and that life must be lived to the fullest.

I started my personal development journey, discovered entrepreneurship and became a property investor with my husband. Based in the South East, our award winning businesses SB Relocations Ltd and SB Walls & More Ltd count numerous successful long-term collaborations with both investors, landlords, tenants and contractors relocating in the South East.

Having founded and grown my two property businesses while expecting a baby and working full-time, I envision coaching and empowering more women to get out of the 'not good enough' mentality that a lot of us experience and help more women to discover how powerful they truly are!

After being inspired by the stories of wonderful Queens in the last two books in this series – Time To Reign and Determined To Rise – I felt a desire to do my part and tell my story, with the hope that it can be of inspiration to female entrepreneurs in the same way that the other stories have been for me. It is an honour being able to contribute.

I dedicate my chapter to my baby boy, Lorenzo, who is my biggest blessing and my biggest why. To my husband, Michele, for always having my back and being there for me. To my family, for always believing in me.

"When *you respect* what you have to say, others will too"

Carrie Griffiths
The Speaking Queen

Still I Rise

Marjorie Peters
Founder
It's Written In The Stars (Alchemy Healing)

"You can knock me down, but I get up twice as strong."
– Sir Lewis Hamilton

Trigger warning[1]

How many times have you been knocked down? How many times has life thrown curveballs and challenges at you? If you're reading this, you've probably already bounced back and you're probably even stronger than before.

See, what I've learned, is that life throws you curveballs and challenges to help you get out of your comfort zone and grow. It's that simple! When you start to learn the dance of life, it becomes a waltz!

But let me tell you, boy have I been thrown a BIG one! And this one woke me up, shook my world and robbed my inner peace. You see, as women, we are given the gift to bring life into this world. And it is expected of us to do so. But what do you do when life decides otherwise? What do you say to yourself and to others when you're not able to fulfil your end of the bargain? It becomes a little complicated right?

---

[1] Suicidal ideation

And then you start to lose self-confidence, lower your self-worth, start to hate yourself, hate your body, distance yourself from the world out there and finally, question your existence and decide that life is not worth living anymore – at least that was the case for me. That was one of the bigger curveballs that life decided to throw at me. After everything that I've been through during childhood, I didn't see this one coming.

Not too long ago, I came to terms with life and said, "Look, if this is what I have to go through, so be it!" Having this attitude and accepting the lessons that I needed to learn in life put me back on the path that I was meant to take. One of the greatest lessons I've learned is that when you can handle uncertainty, it becomes a game changer. In any case, if we look at the bigger picture, nothing is certain in life, except death.

So here's my story... I've been trying to conceive for seven years and failed. 2019 was the last straw when I decided that I was not going to continue with IVF as it was too painful, stressful, and my body was suffering in agony due to the amount of procedures and medication I was taking.

I put on eight kilograms and I felt so unattractive. I had to size up my clothes a number of times. I was a mess as my hormones were raging all over. Different emotions would arise at any given time, and I had no control over them. At times I would just sit and cry and at other times, I would feel depressed and question, why is this happening to me?

I began to shut people out of my life, including my family and friends as I could not take the pressure of being asked, "Any good news?" It was a question that I dreaded. I even had to take myself off social media as I could not read posts of others announcing their good news of being pregnant or showing pictures of their newborn.

I avoided family functions and friends that had children. I became a loner, messed up in my own world. I could not tell night from day. I was practically like a walking zombie. My world was just going to the IVF clinic and home. The only people I saw or interacted with were the nurses and doctors at the clinic. The only comfort I got was eating my favourite food and binge watching Netflix.

At some point, I even got sick of this routine, but in my world there was nothing I could do about it. That was the toxic mindset I had. I was also angry with the doctors at the clinic because my infertility was classified as unknown. This meant that there was nothing I could do to improve my reproductive system except to just keep trying.

I thought to myself that it would be better to know what's wrong and find the solution, but that was not the case. The only thing I had was hope – and that failed me as well.

I remember an incident where a random woman asked me how many children I have, assuming that I was already a mother due to my age. I could not even begin to believe what I was being asked. I became numb and my mouth just couldn't utter a single word to reply to her. That day, I cried my eyes out and was so angry with the whole world. I thought to myself that people can sometimes be very insensitive to others' feelings. I felt everyone and everything was against me. It was one bad luck after another.

This is when I made the decision to quit the IVF treatments. I decided that I'm going to move on in life and forget the whole nightmare. Nothing seemed to be working out in my favour. Somehow deep down in me I believed that if God or the universe wanted to give me the blessings of a child, He would have done it. So I decided to accept my fate that it's not going to happen and move on.

What I didn't realise at the time was that I moved on without healing my trauma. I was not aware that emotions needed to be healed – especially when they're traumatic. In my mind, moving forward was already a great step to take. So I believed…

Some months down the line, the panic attacks started. At first, I couldn't make out what I was experiencing. I didn't recognise the emotions as they were new. I started to google my symptoms and most of it revealed that what I was experiencing was panic attacks. I couldn't believe it at first. I thought I was doing good and moving forward, how could I be getting panic attacks?

What I discovered later down the line was that I was in denial. Eventually the attacks started to get worse. It was borderline out of control. I felt like I was going to die every time I experienced it and I started to have the fear of dying. I remember that I would be driving and having a good day and suddenly it would just resurface and there was nothing I could do about it. There were occasions when I had to pull up at the side of the road as I could not control what I was feeling. I would get about two to three panic attacks in a week and every time it came, my world would just close up around me and it felt like an endless nightmare, except I wasn't asleep.

These episodes continued for over a year. I was fighting for my life and couldn't find a way out. There was no help available for women in my condition except for psychologists and psychiatrists, which was not something I could resonate with or settle for. I knew I didn't want to be on medication for my condition. So I turned to yoga and meditation as I read online that it would help to relieve the symptoms, but unfortunately in my case, nothing worked.

At this point, the fear in me was so great that I thought to myself, I can't live like this anymore. I would rather die and be at ease. So I decided that I was going to take my own life. This thought lingered in my mind for a couple of weeks.

Turning Point
Then, on an autumn night as I was lying on my couch while the TV was on in the background, I started to think of the best and easiest way to end my life. Should I just take a bunch of pills or should I just slit my wrist and go off slowly?

I was also thinking that I didn't want to inconvenience anyone too much when they discovered my body. As all these thoughts were going through my mind and I was playing out the different scenarios in my head, suddenly Sir Lewis Hamilton appeared on the TV saying, "Never give up your hopes and dreams."

As I heard this, I was in sudden shock, it was a light bulb moment for me. Something shifted.

I ran to my back garden and broke down. I sobbed like a baby while thinking to myself, how can I even consider taking my own life? I felt so sorry for myself and to a certain extent, ashamed. It was as if I was in a dream and had suddenly woken up from the nightmare. This is when I asked God for help.

Before this, I never reached out to God as I was angry with Him for not answering my prayers. This was the first time I said out loud, "HELP ME!" From this point on I decided that I was going to take control of my life again and I was willing to do whatever it took for me to get back on track.

I asked God for a sign. I said to Him, "Show me the way." Minutes later as I scrolled through Instagram, I saw a post that read, Real Success Summit: Sign up to watch Deepak Chopra and many other speakers LIVE.

I immediately signed up! I had a gut feeling that this was the sign given to me.

Attending that summit was a turning point in my life. I signed up for different courses, choosing speakers that resonated with me. I was excited to be on this new journey.

For the next six months, I focused on my growth. I shut the world out and for the first time, focused on me, myself and I. I felt empowered and began to believe a new me was emerging… bold, strong, determined and courageous! On this new journey, Sir Lewis Hamilton became my inspiration. I started to follow him on social media along with his races around the world. What I realised is that we shared the same values and beliefs. I became his fan.

All my life, I was always making decisions based on what other people would want me to do or what was the 'right' thing to do, based on society's conformity. This new decision to focus on myself brought me to a different level. It felt like I was creating a new version of me. In fact I even told my family that this is Marj 2.0.

Along this new journey, I started to follow my intuition and heart. I started to become more authentic and spiritual. I connected with my inner and higher self. This flourished beautifully and I started to receive guidance.

The path slowly unfolded and this new person that I got to know was sweet, kind, generous, humble, and most of all filled with love. This was a side of me that I had shut out for many years due to past hurt and experiences. I had been wearing a mask and I had put up barriers in order to protect myself from being hurt again. Fear can really make one stone cold.

After all these barriers were broken down, I came to a point where I realised that I didn't need anyone's approval to be myself. I was okay with not being liked. Reaching this level of authenticity was liberating. I had never felt so alive before. And I've never loved myself as much as I do now. I now know that I come first (not in a selfish way). I've built a beautiful relationship with myself. I must stress here that it wasn't easy but it was so worth it.

Then one day, as I was out for a run, I heard this voice telling me that I needed to share my journey with others. I completed my run, took a shower and then started filming. It was as if it was so natural for me to just take my phone, record a video and post it on Instagram.

After I did this, I came out of the state and asked myself what did I just do? It felt as if I was hypnotised. I couldn't believe I had just posted a video. I've watched many videos of other influencers and always thought to myself how nice it would be to be able to just sit and talk in front of a camera so naturally. Now here I was posting my first video and it happened so suddenly without even planning or getting content together.

Today, I have over one hundred videos on my social media, paying it forward to help others out there who are stuck, disempowered, suffering in pain or discouraged. Doing this led me to start my business and take my life to the next level

I Can See Clearly Now

Being on this new journey made me realise that everything happens for a reason. Today, I see my unknown infertility as a blessing in disguise. I still have hope that one day I will become a mother and I know the universe is already working on that because now I know that I get to create the life that I want.

I also know it's not about me anymore, there's a bigger picture and purpose here. The beautiful part in all of this is that I did not look for my purpose, my purpose found me. This has become my mission to help, heal, and empower other women out there that are going through or have already been through similar challenges as I did.

Whilst on this journey, I also started to cut things out that didn't serve me anymore. This included my limiting beliefs, self-doubt, self-sabotage, people pleasing and my unhealthy eating habits. I started to pay more attention to my health and overall wellbeing. I practised self-care through meditation, exercise, and adopted good eating habits. I changed my environment and the people I mixed with. I cannot begin to stress how important it is to be in the right environment when it comes to transforming and levelling up in life. I distanced myself from toxic people and relationships. I surround myself with like-minded people who add value to my growth and outlook in life. I even ended my marriage as I started to be honest with myself about what brings me joy and passion.

I raised my standards and started to feel empowered. I put myself first before anything else. I ensured that my overall well-being is a priority. I started to feel alive again. My passion came back and my growth just kept on increasing. I knew what I wanted and I was focused on achieving it. I felt reborn, and I even got a tattoo of a phoenix to celebrate my rebirth.

Now, I look at fear in the face and I dance with it. The problem with fear is that we put labels on things of what is 'good' and what is 'bad', but the truth of the matter is it's only an emotion. When we are able to control our emotions and not let them control us, it changes the game. Energies shift and the universe works in your favour. You attract what you embody.

Now, I flow with the current of life as I have been swimming upstream for a very long time and it got tiring. As soon as I was able to surrender to life and flow with it, the game changed. The challenges that came my way were lessons for me to learn and grow to become the person I am today. Every challenge that I faced, I asked myself what can I learn from this? What is life trying to teach me here? It is important to note here that asking the right questions will give you the right answers.

I also learned that everything is energy, and once we're able to understand this concept, we can create the things that we want. This is where manifestation comes into play. You can create the life of your dreams by just shifting your energy and raising your vibration. I'm a strong believer in the universe and its powers. When I say you can have everything you dream of and more, I mean it because I'm the living proof of it. When you start to work on yourself first, creating the foundation for everything that is to come, you are rooting and setting yourself up to win. You become more focused on your goals and start to see results.

Only after I built my foundation, did I decide to start my business. I knew it was crucial for me to be in the right state of mind before anything else. I had to heal myself first before I could heal others. I can safely say that today, I'm living my best life. My journey may have just begun, but all the wisdom and knowledge that I have learned from my challenges in the past takes me to a whole different level moving forward. I am blessed and grateful for the past and its lessons, and I look forward to the future. Still I rise…

In my business, I help women that are specifically going through a challenging time while undergoing IVF treatments or women that have gone through IVF treatments and are still childless.

I have been down that road and I know what it feels like to be in such a situation. I know and recognise all the setbacks, triggers, emotional turmoil, disappointments, trauma, fears and confusion. It's a tough journey and sadly this issue is not addressed enough because many women suffer in silence. We are not used to or maybe even not comfortable talking about our struggles when it comes to our infertility.

This is the reason why I have made it my mission and calling to create more awareness on the severity of this issue and to help other women on similar journeys to overcome their pain and suffering. I work through one-on-one coaching tailored to individuals based on a step-by-step process. Through my experience and wisdom, I've developed a methodology called S.T.A.R.S. It is tailored for women mentioned above, but not limited to others as this methodology works with all individuals. It is the basic foundation for creating a better version of yourself and living your best life.

S.T.A.R.S. Methodology:
The **S** represents Self-Love. I believe that before you can start anything, you must first look at yourself and evaluate where you are at. This brings clarity and understanding to get to where you want to go.

By practising self-love, you start to build a strong foundation from within. Along this journey, you will discover your greatness, gifts, passion, talents, and much more. This is also the stage where healing takes place. You become more in tune with your emotions, feelings and your body. The inner world always reflects the outer world.

The **T** represents Thoughts. This second step helps to shift the mindset and cultivate positive thinking whilst clearing away all limiting beliefs, trauma, triggers, fears, and self-doubt. The mind is a beautiful tool if controlled and used in the right way.

It's also a good time to start practising gratitude with an abundance mindset. The more grateful we are, the more abundant we feel. By discarding all your limiting beliefs, trauma, fears, triggers, and self-doubt you start to believe the impossible and you become empowered.

The **A** represents Actions. After having a mindset shift, it's time to go forward and take action. This includes working out or exercising, meditation, yoga, etc. All these body movements and stillness helps to build energy and raise your vibration. When energy and vibration levels increase, the mind has clarity. This helps you make better decisions and keeps the mind focused.

Taking action also includes setting your goals, intention and having a vision of moving forward in life. Some of the questions to ask yourself are:

- What are your dreams?
- What are you passionate about?
- What do you love doing if you could choose your career or perhaps own a business?

The **R** represents Respond. The idea here is to be able to respond and not react. Once a strong mindset is built, one feels empowered and gains courage to overcome any challenges or barriers. This allows the mind to think and see things from a different perspective. When you change your perspective, you change your life. Responding and not reacting to a certain situation changes the game and creates more opportunities.

The **S** represents Serve. I'm a strong believer in growth and contribution. This is a time of reflection on all the accomplishments and work you put into yourself, looking back at how you've healed and looking at life from a different perspective, equipped with a positive mindset. The journey empowers you to share your knowledge and wisdom by helping others. This also includes giving back to your community and volunteering.

About Me

I'm Marjorie, Founder of It's Written In The Stars (Alchemy Healing) based in London. Not too long ago, I discovered that I have special gifts that I didn't know I had in me. I learnt that I'm a Starseed.

For those of you who are not familiar with what a Starseed is, it's actually a person with an old soul that has special gifts. Starseeds help make the world a better place. One of the gifts I have is the gift of healing. I am able to sense the energies around me and also feel a person's energy. By using my energy and transmitting it outwards by light, I am able to heal energies that are heavy. And so this has become my journey and mission: to heal others. I use this gift along with the wisdom, knowledge, and experience I have in my business.

I'm also a professional public speaker, one of the many other talents I discovered about myself. The reason I took up public speaking is to advocate for women and to empower them. I believe that when women come together, mountains can be moved.

I would like to thank Queens In Business Club for this amazing opportunity to share my story. My dear reader, I hope that this chapter has inspired you to never give up on life. When you are faced with challenges, remember that life is the greatest teacher you'll ever have. If you give it a chance, it will teach you all its magic and glory. It will fill your cup with eternal wisdom and grace.

This chapter is dedicated to the person who saved my life. You are my angel on earth and my soulmate from past lives and beyond...

Shim Ravalia's Crown Of Courage

Shim Ravalia

Founder

The Gut Intuition

"Courage starts with showing up and letting ourselves be seen." – Brene Brown

What does courage mean to me?

Bluntly and directly put, to have the lady balls to stand up to fear, pain, difficulties and sh*t that life tends to throw at you, with unshakeable strength. Let's face it, everything happens for a reason. Why? Because you need to learn a thing or two to get to the next level (whatever that may be) and be the version of yourself you are meant to be.

That's why I believe in facing life challenges with a dollop of courage and a sprinkle of bravery. It's not always easy, but here's a little secret I use to help me stand tall in the face of fear...

Shim's Crown Of Courage

1. <u>Bravery</u>

The first spike on my Crown Of Courage stands for bravery. It's the 'getting up, feeling the fear and pooping your pants' kind of feeling (hopefully not literally) and doing it anyway. Back in 2012, I made that brave decision to leave the employed world with all the benefits and safety nets that I had stored away for a rainy day and charged forward, going from full-time employed to a business owner in less than 30 days. It was scary as hell because I didn't have a business name set up, no website, no logo, not even a name registered with Companies House, let alone a location to work from.

Crazy, right?

Well, I could have easily talked myself out of it and gone back to my full-time job giving myself the excuses of why I couldn't start my own business. But I really believed in myself that I could do it and guess what? I did. 10 years of being a business owner later ... well, the results speak for themselves.

Now, I'm not saying go out there and put your big girl pants on and take a massive leap into the unknown. My advice to you is just tune into your own abilities and bravery and dig deep on what you want to do. For me, I was tired of the same old sh*t every day; it stifled my creativity. I was bored and I was desperate for a fresh outlook for my career and what truly made me feel happy and fulfilled. That stuff right there is what truly matters!

2. Speaking Up

When you become more known in what you do and there are more eyeballs on you than normal, you will get a handful of green eyed monsters that will tend to get a little jealous of your success. I have two words for them, it begins with an F and ends in an F. Just kidding! This is what my ego would like to say, however it's important in situations like this to come with love, compassion and kindness.

In a way, what's really happening here is that you've inspired and triggered something in that person that they wish they had. But what they don't realise is that they are limiting themselves, not you. Don't be afraid to speak up for yourself, own it and move on, particularly if it's a very toxic situation. It takes courage to do so but in my experience, LOVE WINS EVERY TIME.

3. Taking Risks

Playing safe and too small against what you know deep down you are capable of, doesn't help you or the other people you want to serve. Taking a risk sometimes gets a bad rap, however do your due diligence when it comes to the risks you want to take.

Ultimately, get cosy with taking risks and get to know each other. A bit like a warm campfire toasting your marshmallows and a guitar playing in the background. Sounds epic doesn't it?

Whether the risk is calculated or not, look at the pros and cons but importantly, does the risk line up with your values and vision for what you want to achieve? Does it contribute to your legacy?

Just spending good quality time on this section helped me massively in moving forward with my businesses and connections and saved me a lot of time, redirecting it to where it needed to be spent.

When you are faced with risks, it means you are alive, awake, and pushing away from the norm. You are LIVING!

Trust me, it's worth it!

4. <u>Growth</u>

Growth is a painful process but a beautiful journey. I'd rather go through the pain of growth knowing that on the other side of it, a better version of me is ready to greet the world. To be honest, everything I'm talking to you about right now screams growth so welcome it with both arms.

I spoke a lot about growth in Queens In Business' last book, Determined To Rise, so if you haven't read it yet, I'd go and read that as well to give you a much needed boost when it comes to the wonderful world of growth.

I know growth is painful, that's why courage is there to give it a cuddle ;)

5. <u>Change</u>

Me and change are best friends and have been for a long time. I mean all I had to do to realise change and celebrate it is look at all the picture albums my dear mum had put together over time. It made me realise how much I've changed for the better and actually how far I've come. Change is the one thing that is constant all of the time. Change is one of my top three core values in life, business and in health.

So block some time out, look at old pictures of your journey and celebrate with a big beautiful smile on your face :)

6. <u>Leadership</u>

Oooooo now getting to the serious stuff! Ten years ago when I entered the world of business, I was not thinking about leadership, leading others or myself, or to lead in general. Even though I went from employed to business owner, I realised I was creating a business from an employed mindset! I learnt that the hard way and I don't want that to happen to you too.

What is leadership? Simply put, leadership is when direction is set, the vision is at the forefront and you're doing the right thing for the greater good. Leadership is all about mapping out where we need to go as a team to 'win' as a team and achieve our mission, vision and goals. While it's really exciting to set the direction and the wheels are in motion, as a leader you've got to manage a team, conflicts, challenges and more to get your business and people to the right destination in the most efficient and effective way possible.

Leadership is a responsibility. You can't fall into the trap of the 'blame game' here. People in your life look up to you for direction, inspiration and faith. I could have written 'hope' here, but when it comes to leadership, hope is not what it takes to achieve the results you want.

Trust is something you have to get comfortable with. And I'm not talking about trusting others. What I mean is seriously looking at yourself in the mirror and asking yourself... "Does my behaviour encourage and instill trust?"

Listen well and I mean really well! Be open and accountable. There will be drama and criticism along the way but don't forget the bigger picture.

So to zoom out and tell you what courage has really taught me, it is to...

Be brave to really lead, and in order to lead, speak up to create change, and to create lasting change, take risks. The best of it all is that risk equals growth which brings it back to...

YOU.

As you can see from my Crown Of Courage, the middle of the crown is essentially you. Your unique traits and characteristics make up you, that holds the crown together nice and straight. So look after yourself inside out, make self-care a priority and be selfish for the right reasons because lovely, you are an original, always.

Now time to get a little creative and create your own Crown Of Courage! I've put together a list of different traits and characteristics that could fit together to build courage in the following diagram. Go ahead and circle the ones you feel resonate with you.

• Self-Discipline	• Dependable	• Creative
• Authenticity	• Integrity	• Balanced
• Resilient	• Expressive	• Respectful
• Humble	• Grounded	• Fearless
• Emotional Intelligence	• Encouraging	• Grateful
• Committed	• Trustworthy	• Inspirational
• Daring	• Growth	• Wise
• Risk Taker	• Confident	• Energetic
• Leader	• Certain	• Rule Breaker
• Calm	• Adaptable	• Intuitive
• Caring	• Perseverance	• Don't Settle
• Decisive	• Driven	• Purposeful
• Strength	• Accountable	• Humility
• Truth Seeker	• Assertive	• Brave
• Honest	• Focused	• Bold
• Visionary	• Open-Minded	• Curious
• Supportive	• Empowering	• Patience

Not listed? Don't worry, just write it below:

_____

_____

Now that you've circled your traits and characteristics for courage, create your own Crown Of Courage by adding your top six traits and characteristics to it. Have fun with it, take a picture and place it somewhere where you can see it everyday.

It looks really good on you ;)

My Crown Of Courage

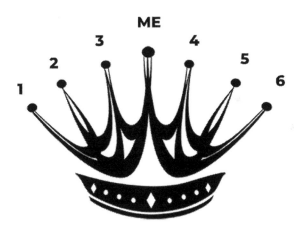

1 -

2 -

3 -

4 -

5 -

6 -

Looks Good On Me!

About Me

I am the Founder of The Gut Intuition and Head of Operations & Growth for the Queens In Business Club. I help business owners and entrepreneurs go from stress to unlimited energy and razor sharp focus without burning out in health and in business.

I've had the pleasure of being featured in many well-known publications like Business Woman Today, CBS News, Fox, NBC and ABC to really spread my message and my vision about health for the future of entrepreneurs all over the world.

Born and bred in East London, I have always been curious about the human body and the mind. I came away from university with two degrees in Sports Rehabilitation and from here I worked in gyms and leisure centres until I found my entrepreneurial path.

Having been an entrepreneur for over 10 years now, I have overcome many hurdles and challenges that many entrepreneurs face along the way. I hope that this book gives you the much needed guidance to stand tall, be brave and be courageous enough to handle whatever may come your way.

Petrified But Getting On With It!

Michelle Walker-Smith
Founder
Aqua Lettings Ltd

"Turn your wounds into wisdom." – Oprah Winfrey

During the early part of 2009, my GP told me that what had happened to me generally only happens on soap operas. I just felt relieved that I was alive…

To give you a bit of background, I'd always done okay with things – owned my own house, had loads of friends, had a decent job, company car – and yet I always felt like I was still lacking something. I guess it was that entrepreneurial flair within me, although at the time I hadn't realised it.

At nineteen years old, I did Camp America and became a swimming instructor on Long Island, New York for the summer. At twenty-three, while I was studying for my degree, I completed BUNAC. This is where you travel abroad (I chose Toronto, Canada) and I had to find a job as well as source accommodation once there. I was petrified for both but did them anyway! This enabled me to travel and see a bit of the world, which I love to do.

Fast forward to 2001, I met my now husband, Peter, who is originally from the West Midlands. I've always been a home bird but, ultimately, when the long-distance relationship got the better of us, I moved to the West Midlands to join him. Again, this petrified me but I just got on with it!

As my job was in housing management, I found another role quite quickly. A year passed and I hated it there, I found it such an oppressive place. Luckily, Peter was happy to move back up to the North East. He tried to explain that if we remortgaged his house (where we lived in the Midlands) and remortgaged my house (I'd rented that out up North), we'd be able to buy a third property. The neighbours up North probably heard my screams of fear from the Midlands!

I totally did not understand this concept. Buy two get one free?! (Boy, do I wish I'd known then what I know now!) I was petrified – but we did it anyway (a common theme, right?).

We bought our third house for cash – we both had company cars – and we lived like DINKYs (Dual Income No Kids). Life was good.

Although it wasn't in my historical housing management field, the job I got back up North dealt with tenants – in a house refurbishment sense. Resident Liaison was my title.

And then I went for a promotion and it all went pear-shaped.

Middle management seemed to take a dislike towards me – I still to this day do not know why. They made my life hell. I'm a sensitive soul and did take things very much to heart. I tried so hard to please but it seemed the harder I tried, the worse it got. I lost confidence, my anxiety shot through the roof, and I hated the job I once loved. I ended up getting a written warning – which I appealed – and it got quashed, but my life was a living hell for months.

If it wasn't for Peter, I don't know what would have happened. He gave me the confidence to walk away, head held high, knowing they needed me more than I needed them. I was petrified about the future but walked away anyway.

One October evening after I walked out, I treated myself to a Reiki session. That night, in the early hours, I was woken to the most excruciating pain in my abdomen. I couldn't straighten up – painkillers didn't touch it.

That morning, Peter went off to work, then my pain got even worse. My dad had to come up and take me to A&E. I didn't know what was happening.

I was diagnosed with 'stomach flu' but I instinctively knew it was more than that. My mum had a complicated appendicitis and my great grandfather passed away from peritonitis. I'll not go into any gory details but suffice to say, after a few days, my appendix must have exploded causing septicemia, peritonitis, blood and stomach infections. This meant I had to be fed through tubes, was on morphine and all sorts of antibiotics. I vividly remember asking a nurse if I was ever going to get out of the hospital. I remember feeling petrified, but death for me wasn't an option!

I eventually got out of hospital after three weeks and due to the chronic infection, I needed a second operation the following April, once my insides had settled, to remove the remainder of my appendix. At that time, they investigated other damage caused and it was found my fallopian tubes were completely blocked. This was devastating news as we were hoping for a family.

Once I recovered from that surgery, I found an administration job. Life had to go on and I had to come to terms with the fact we may be childless and IVF was to be our only option.

I felt my body had let me down, that I was a failure. However, being someone who never gives up, I pushed through and on our first fresh cycle of IVF, astoundingly I fell pregnant.

Complications

The fear and excitement were insurmountable. My ovaries had been over-stimulated which caused swelling and fluid retention – again, this could have been life threatening, but thankfully I survived. We achieved 20 odd embryos, so we froze a few for a future round.

The pregnancy went relatively smoothly, apart from at the end when I was showing signs of preeclampsia. I was induced and on going into labour in August 2008 it was intense from the onset. The midwives thought I was going to give birth within a couple of hours. Then it was found he was back-to-back and got stuck.

They gave me drugs to stop the labour, then drugs to start the labour. I needed an epidural but nothing was moving him. An emergency caesarean section was the only way. We had constant monitoring from the midwives all the way through and in theatre, we were greeted by a team of around 20 medical staff. I knew it was serious, I was exhausted, petrified, teary, didn't know what to expect and so opted to be put to sleep for the emergency C-Section.

I woke up to the news that I had a beautiful baby boy. He was born not breathing but thank God he survived his ordeal. He was in an incubator, looking huge compared to all the little dots in the Special Care Baby Unit. He was 9lb 4oz and I named him Nathan.

Apparently, I had needed two blood transfusions and my womb wouldn't contract. The consultant had held my womb in his hand to stitch it up. If that hadn't worked, the only other option would have been a hysterectomy. Thank God he managed to put me back together.

They ran tests on Nathan as he'd been starved of oxygen during birth. As I was recovering, the doctor came into my room with words I shall never forget for as long as I live, "Your baby has a tumour on his heart."

It was found his heart was twice the size it should have been.

At that point, my world fell through the floor. To have gone through everything I had gone through, to finally have my precious baby here, to not knowing if he was going to survive, was the most traumatic news I could ever have imagined.

It felt like a bad dream. I was devastated. Peter had nipped away and my parents were there but they were helpless. I remember listening to a guttural wail and a painful cry – then I realised it was me. I had never experienced pain like it.

Nathan was emergency blue-lighted to the Freeman Hospital in Newcastle-Upon-Tyne, the specialist heart hospital in the North East of England. I was stuck at Wansbeck Hospital recovering myself. There was no way I was going to be apart from my baby, so I discharged myself early – even though I was very poorly.

Nathan spent the first week of his life in hospital. It was such a worrying time. I couldn't bring myself to open the 'new baby' cards, just in case. Due to my wanting to breastfeed, I set alarms throughout the night to express and build a milk bank at the hospital for his feeds. It was a time I'd not wish upon anybody.

Thanks to the amazing team at the Freeman Hospital, and many tests over the coming days, it was found the 'tumour' was thought to be a cardiac fibroma. There was no telling one hundred per cent without surgery, but I had complete faith in the consultant, Richard Kirk. They did all sorts of tests and scans on Nathan, and to this day, the heart unit still monitors him.

Meant To Be

It was so difficult not to be overprotective of a much longed-for precious baby who had been through so much. I sometimes physically had to stop myself from wrapping him up in cotton wool. Through experience, I have learned it is important to give children space to make their own mistakes and learn from their own experiences.

Life still wasn't straightforward for us though. Nathan was only a few weeks old when Peter was made redundant from his business development manager job. The feeling of panic and uncertainty set in. I was on maternity leave, he was the breadwinner – what were we going to do?

An awful feeling to have, not knowing where the next pay check was coming from. It was over this period that I began to appreciate anyone could become homeless, through no fault of their own.

Thankfully, Peter found long-term contractual work in his area of expertise and this seemed a good time to go for our second round of IVF. Amazingly, I fell pregnant again.

The doctors and midwives tried to get me to opt for a natural birth this time. But there was no way I was going to risk another precious baby of mine getting stuck. I can heal from my scars from a C-Section – but we may not have been as fortunate this time during the birth. I stuck to my guns and Jessica arrived safely in November 2010 weighing 8lb 11oz.

She was scanned for a heart defect and remarkably she was clear.

I felt so happy and so blessed to have a boy and a girl. I had always wanted a large family. We went for a third fresh round of IVF which sadly did not take. I was just over forty, so I felt my age was against me. We then used the frozen embryos from 2008 and one took! It was a strange concept to think I was carrying Nathan's twin, four years apart. I had a positive pregnancy test though!

I was elated, although instinctively I knew something was wrong. Unfortunately, I miscarried at around nine weeks. I was devastated as I always dreamed of having three babies. I needed an operation to remove the little baby, then took some time to grieve.

Peter and I looked to adopt a little one. Peter comes from a huge family and although I had no siblings, I'd always dreamed of having a large family. We went through the training, however on completing it, Peter decided he couldn't go through with it. I had to respect that, we had two beautiful babies and had so much to be thankful for, so I accepted that our family was complete.

In the summer of 2014, I noticed my period was late (generally I was as regular as clockwork). I'd said to Peter, "Imagine if I was pregnant." He dismissed it seeing as it was a physical impossibility. I waited another week, then decided to take a test. Yes! You guessed it – the result was positive.

How on earth? Pardon my French but I found that a total mind f*ck. All these years of illness, infertility, IVF, miscarriage – then BAM! Pregnant through natural methods. I'd heard that often women fall pregnant when their infertility was due to unknown circumstances – once their minds are off it, the body relaxes and so on. However, my infertility was due to my tubes being blocked – a physical diagnosis. No wrigglers were getting through my bad boys! Or so I thought.

I bled several times throughout this pregnancy, I thought I'd lost him on numerous occasions. Even on holiday in Spain where I ended up visiting the hospital, then having a follow-up appointment to see the little embryo growing, fighting to be in there. He was a medical miracle – meant to be. Patrick arrived through C-Section in March 2015 weighing in at 8lbs.

He was scanned for any heart abnormalities, and one was found – WITHIN his heart. WTF. This was diagnosed as something that could cause a stroke in later life. The only way of avoiding this was for him to potentially have open heart surgery. What were we meant to do? Our precious baby boy, who was a medical miracle. I felt he was meant to be here – then to be presented that at a few weeks old, he was potentially going to have his heart stopped, the tumour removed, then his heart started again, the risks felt catastrophic. How could we make a decision like that?

I asked our new consultant at the time what he would do in my situation, he said he'd probably get the surgery done to alleviate the future risk. However, following various meetings, I didn't have much confidence in him. Sometimes it was difficult to get a straight answer out of him, he was vague and indecisive when you asked a direct question. I wasn't convinced about leaving the fate of my little boy in his hands. I vividly remember Peter and I sitting flicking a coin to decide our son's fate. Then did the best of three flicks (they were all saying leave it in there). I couldn't believe our son's fate was being decided with the flick of a coin.

Not being one to give up easily, I decided to find Richard Kirk (the consultant who dealt with Nathan's condition). He had moved on from the Freeman Hospital and I remembered someone saying he had gone to America. I didn't know what exactly he was doing but I made it my mission to find him. I searched all over social media looking for him, I googled him and found medical papers he'd written, and I emailed people who were mentioned in his papers. I literally searched all night.

Success! I managed to get in touch. Richard Kirk was in Dallas. Once I had made contact, he agreed to help and I arranged with our hospital to send him copies of the results from Patrick's MRI (and Nathan's historic scan details). He researched and asked his team in the USA and the conclusion was that it was the same condition as Nathan has, a cardiac fibroma, sited in a different place.

Relieved was an understatement. Obviously, there's always something at the back of my mind about my two boys having 'extra bits' (as I call them) on their hearts, but to know it was unlikely that open heart surgery was necessary was a tremendous relief. All the way along this nightmare, I told myself my precious babies couldn't be taken away from me. Thank God they weren't.

It's All In The Mind
Prior to Patrick being born, Peter's current contract had ended. He was absolutely fed up with other people deciding when he was and wasn't going to work.

He had always been interested in property and so in January 2015, Peter attended an introductory weekend at Progressive Property called Multiple Streams of Property. Unbeknown to me, he signed up to what was then called VIP, a 12-month property-based mastermind, taking him away from the family once a month – the family of soon-to-be three children, aged seven and under.

We had only a little income stream from our rentals. I was on maternity pay via the government as I'd reduced my hours to suit having the family. Peter was like a man on speed when he came back from his weekend. He'd had so many lightbulb moments. This was going to be our future, the way forward.

You can imagine – me eight months heavily' pregnant, hormonal, very risk averse and scared. Who were these Progressive Property people? Who was this ROB MOORE character?

We argued, I cried – almost gave birth – divorced him – and killed him all at once! He'd used our three months of mortgage/bills money we had… on a course… A FECKIN COURSE!

Eventually I succumbed to allowing him to stay in the house and gave him 12 months to show me this was going to work.

Looking back, it did all happen for a reason. Due to the fact we had no income, we HAD to make this work. We made a joint venture agreement with Peter's brother and sister to re-mortgage their mum and dad's house to release some equity. Peter researched our goldmine area, Ashington in Northumberland. He'd historically worked there so knew it well. I'd worked in housing management there in my younger years and almost had a fit when I heard we were going to invest there! I was petrified but we did it anyway and Peter sourced and purchased 13 properties in 12 months.

I was reserved, this was totally alien to me. Getting into debt, spending other people's money, using credit cards for refurbishments… in theory, it sounded too good to be true.

I was on maternity leave and wanted to enjoy my baby, so we decided to use a local agent, but the houses weren't getting let quick enough. Excuses of summer holidays and the like were branded around but in my history of housing management, people need housing every day of the year.

We also investigated a joint venture with a local agent, however she changed her mind which was fair enough, but it had clarified in my head what I wanted to do. I ended up testing the water and advertising, then actually finding tenants myself. I then had a decision to make – did I return to my admin position or continue letting properties myself?

The fear of the unknown was horrendous and after a few sleepless nights later I chose the unknown, and Aqua Lettings Ltd was born.

Me, risk averse? I was ADAMANT I was going to make this work.

I was feeling quite good about life. Managing to let our houses to people who desperately needed them. Looking past their credit files and history and looking at them individually, learning how they got into bad situations and building trust with them to move them forward into housing. I knew from first-hand experience how easy it was to get into debt. Some of my first tenants are still with me now.

Peter was still on VIP and the business grew organically as investors were introduced into the Aqua Lettings way, and their houses were managed and tenanted too. Then through Peter's networking, he met new business partners and got opportunities to explore commercial conversion. I was hesitant as we hadn't grown Aqua enough to be self-sufficient, but these things never show up at a 'good' time.

Peter's development experience stood him in good stead and he felt confident. I was petrified but went along with it. However, as with all new things, there were things he could have done differently.

Fast forward five years or so, we were left in tens of thousands of pounds worth of debt. One project had problems with the investor and one project involved Peter getting sacked as a director. There had been a distinct personality conflict there with the other two directors being friends from the past (two's company, three is a crowd).

We'd had no income from any of these projects. I thought one of the projects in particular was a no-brainer and was going to achieve a six-figure outcome at the end of it. How wrong could I be?

Peter's confidence hit an all-time low, it even affected his physical health let alone his mental health. He ended up with a blood clot and collapsed. This was all put down to stress. Luckily, he recovered, but what on earth were we going to do?

I went to the doctors and asked for something to get me through. My anxiety had shot through the roof. I had such a mixture of emotions running through me. Even though I knew logically that Peter hadn't done this intentionally, I blamed him. Putting our family at risk, risking our properties. If they had been taken by one of the creditors, I would never have forgiven him. We had stupidly used credit cards as he had not had much of an income, and we needed to refurbish some of our portfolios. In total, we had around £100K worth of debt. How the hell were we going to get out of this one?

Peter had completely lost his mojo. A different partnership he was working on dissolved due to his lack of enthusiasm and motivation. I was angry and disappointed, he could have done a load of deal sourcing to at least make a dent in this debt, but I think he was depressed. He had had the stuffing well and truly knocked out of him.

At the same time, I had been working on personal self-development and my mindset. I had also reached rock bottom and if it wasn't for my precious babies, I really don't know where I would have been.

I tried to enrol Peter on various mindset training – I wanted my hero back.

Over a few weeks, I gave myself a good talking to. Why should I rely on Peter (or anyone for that matter) for my happiness? What gives me the right to try to change someone? I was on various masterminds and discussed things with mentors and peers and I reached out to Rob Moore, who gave me some invaluable advice.

Rob put things into perspective for me. I realised I was going to have to carry us forward, it was down to me. I made it my mission to grow my lettings business and make us more financially stable. I suggested selling our family home to release the equity, we ended up renting it out which enabled us to obtain the equity but also was a huge benefit to us through the rent obtained. We sold Peter's house in the West Midlands as it was too far away to manage anyway. We slowly chipped away at the debt.

Aqua Lettings is growing, as I believed it would. It is all so much down to mindset. We are almost out of debt now, all through our property portfolio, growing the Aqua Lettings business and my new business ventures.

All this really does work.

Over the years, so much has been thrown in my direction. I could have given up and played the victim, but what example would I have been giving my children? How would I have felt if I'd just given up?

If you embrace and appreciate what you have you will have an abundant life. If you feel you aren't good enough, or you don't have enough, this will be mirrored back to you.

It has taken me determination, a complete change of mindset, sheer grit, and perseverance to get me to where I am. And I'm not done yet...

About Me

I have always been a people person and today, I believe that everyone can build businesses from scratch and take control of their happiness.

At the age of twenty-four, I completed my business degree and secured a position in housing management, where I helped and worked with people to ensure their houses became a home.

Things then took a turn for the worse when at the age of thirty-five, I suffered an undiagnosed burst appendix which resulted in peritonitis and septicemia, causing infertility, and almost dying.

However, with sheer courage and determination, I have gone on to have three beautiful children, the eldest two through IVF and the third as a medical miracle!

Fast forward to the age of forty-three when I discovered the world of entrepreneurship and became an investor with my husband, Peter. Shortly after starting a property portfolio, I set up the award-winning Aqua Lettings Ltd, which has an outstanding reputation in the North East, with both landlords and tenants, for always going the extra mile.

I always give back wherever possible and today I run a successful property mentoring company too, helping others who wish to get started in the property industry. In my story, I share with you how with sheer grit, determination, and courage – anything is possible.

My chapter is dedicated to two men who have touched my life more than they will ever know.

Professor Richard Kirk MA FRCP FRCPCH – who at the time was Consultant Pediatric Cardiologist at the Freeman Hospital, Newcastle upon Tyne. Thank you from the bottom of my heart, you were there to guide me through two of the worst times in my life.

Rob Moore, entrepreneur, investor, author, podcaster, public speaking world record holder and Founder of The Rob Moore Foundation. Thank you, I really appreciate your time and guidance. Without you, I would not be the person I am today.

"Sometimes, courage is the ability to stay still or *persevere*"

Sunna Coleman
The Writing Queen

If I Can Do It, So Can You

Dorothy Ewels
Fiction Author and Writing Coach
The Write Support

"Whether you think you can, or you think you can't – you're right." – Henry Ford

Trigger Warning[1]

I'm no stranger to loss, but it wasn't always that way. I started life with challenges, it's true, but none that would prepare me for what was to come as an adult.

Born in the 70s with a rare genetic skin condition that labelled me a Butterfly Child[2], my parents protected me. While I know they did it from a place of love, it left me woefully unprepared for adulthood. On the flip side though, the lessons I learned taught me so much about myself and the gifts locked inside of me, just waiting to be unleashed.

I'd like to share my journey to freedom with you.

Wayne Dyer said, "Don't die with your music still in you". I've embraced his wisdom, choosing to share my version of that music with the world. But first I had to overcome the obstacles life threw my way on my path to becoming a published author.

---

[1] Suicidal ideation
[2] Children born with Epidermolysis Bullosa, a rare genetic skin condition, are often called "Butterfly Children" because their skin seems as fragile as a butterfly's wing.

The First Time: Fear, Depression, Anxiety

Please be awake. I need you.

The litany played on a loop in my head as I drove through the quiet of the night. Fear, depression, anxiety – they'd been my constant companions for weeks, never silent. Not even for a moment.

But I'm getting ahead of myself. Let's start at the beginning.

My birthday dawned grim and miserable. I was turning thirty – no longer would I be able to say I was in my twenties and something about that depressed me more than it had a right to. But that wasn't the worst of it. It was the day my husband and I finally had to admit defeat.

We'd sunk our entire life savings into a business that had seemed so promising. Having done our due diligence, weighing all the pros and cons, we took what we'd thought was a calculated risk. In our trusting naïveté, we'd never once stopped to consider that the owners would falsify the documents to get the business – their dying business – sold.

Yet here we were less than a year later, flogging a dead horse, having sunk everything we had into keeping it alive.

An enormous sense of failure hung over me. Guilt at having to let our three staff members go ate at me twenty-four seven. And now, I was thirty. My life sucked. Depression and anxiety sat like a lead balloon in the pit of my stomach and fear was soon to add itself to the nasty mix.

Creditors began knocking at the door, phoning and sending lawyers letters. It was a waking nightmare. The once outgoing, confident woman I'd been, began to disappear by degrees. Until one morning, months after this insanity had begun, I woke up and she was gone. I was a wreck on the inside, pretending all was well on the outside.

And, apparently, doing a superb job of faking it. No one knew how far I'd been slipping into the bowels of my own personal hell. It wasn't until one particular evening that it all came to a head though. My husband, thankfully, had managed to get his old job back and was working when a knock sounded on our front door at half past nine that night.

Not turning a light on, I peeked out the bedroom window and saw it was, once again, the sheriff of the court coming to serve yet another notice. It was almost a physical feeling as something shifted inside me. As I stood in the dark bedroom, a thought popped into my head.

I had policies that would pay out should anything happen to me. If I were no longer around, I would solve two issues at the same time. I would be free of this nightmare I couldn't seem to escape, and my family would be able to settle all the debt we currently had no way of paying. A win-win situation, to my mind.

I considered this to be the best solution. But something in the far reaches of my brain obviously wasn't on board with this plan because instead of taking action, I loaded my sleeping son into our family car and took a drive. With no particular destination in mind, I cruised the quiet streets on a Sunday night. Few people were out. They were all ensconced in their homes, living their lives.

Without even realising it, I found myself in my best friend's neighbourhood and suddenly the words, "Please be awake. I need you," began to loop in my head. A decision born out of an unconscious sense of survival was made. If she was awake, I'd stop in and visit with her for a while. If not, I would simply go home and do what needed to be done to put my plan in motion.

My sweet boy, so young and innocent, sat quietly in the back seat. My normally chatty seven-year-old, as if sensing all was not well, never uttered so much as a word as we meandered aimlessly through the streets of Cape Town. Pulling into my friend's driveway, an enormous sense of relief washed over me.

Despite the fact it was now ten thirty on a 'school night' my friend's husband invited me in without hesitation. Maybe my face gave away the fact that something wasn't right, or maybe it was because it was so late on a Sunday night – whatever it was – I will forever be grateful to both of them.

She led me down the short hall to her bedroom, closed the door and sat me down. "Hubby's got the kids. This is a safe space. Now, out with it."

The words that followed were, quite probably, the last thing she expected to hear. A look of compassion crossed her face and then things got real. I got the tongue-lashing of my life. When she finally wound down, she finished off with, "I love you more than the moon – you know that, but that's the most selfish thing I've ever heard. Money will never make up for the devastation you'll leave behind if you do this. They need you."

She opened the door and pointed to my son playing in the living room with her two girls. "That little boy needs you, now more than ever. I get things are hard right now, but together you can figure it out. But not if you take the selfish way out."

If not for this amazing woman, I'm certain I wouldn't be here to tell you this story.

The Second Time: Coming Out The Other Side
It took us a few years, but we did it. We came out on the other side, not completely unscathed, but at least we were all okay. I found a part-time job working for a commercial bakery. Slowly we rebuilt our lives, dug our way out from under our debt and, eventually, life settled into a new normal.

Truth be told, I would never be the same person I was before we'd lost our business, but I learned to be a new version of myself. Albeit a more anxious, less trusting version. Slowly but surely, we got back on our feet. There was a sense of accomplishment, having dug ourselves out from under the financial ruin we'd found ourselves in, and I was incredibly grateful to still be here.

The bakery continued to grow and soon we needed a logistics and production manager. It was more money and better hours than where my husband was working so, after discussing it, he decided to apply for the position. Our relationship has always been such that we are able to live and work together quite happily.

Not long after he started working at the bakery, my parents moved in with us as my dad's health began to fail. My mum then joined the company too. For the first time in some time, things felt stable and settled.

Well, there we were, all our eggs in one basket, and wouldn't you know it, with no clue it was coming we had the rug yanked out from under us. Without going into a lot of detail, the owner of the company owed the power company a large debt which he'd made arrangements to pay off over time.

The agreement was that as long as he paid the current balance and a portion of the old debt each month, without skipping a month, all would be well. The first missed payment and the full amount owing would immediately be due and payable.

Yes, you guessed. He skipped a payment.

When the power went off, we contacted him to inform him. We were told to find out if there were any issues – a.k.a. power outages – in our area. But, of course, there weren't any.

Having established it wasn't a power outage but, in fact, a bounced cheque, we let him know the outcome of the conversation. His response? Shut the factory down and send everyone home. Let them know, "I'll be in touch." And that was that.

Once again, we found ourselves, for all intents and purposes, bankrupt. In fact, to this day he's never paid either my husband or myself the outstanding salaries or leave pay he owed us.

This time, though, things were a little different. Having gone through it once, we seemed better able to handle it a second time – better equipped, I guess you could say. I, for one, definitely felt in a far healthier headspace than the first time around. Yes, we were down for a second time but, by God, we weren't out of the game by a long shot this time.

The stars seemed to align for us at just the right moment. Our former boss had found himself employment at a commercial property brokerage and had organised an administrative position for me. I can't say I was thrilled to be back working with him but, as the saying goes, beggars can't be choosers.

As luck would have it, my mother and husband quickly found other work too.

The Third Time: There's A Reason They're Clichés

As a fiction author, you're taught to avoid using clichés in your writing, where possible. But life has taught me that there's a reason they've become clichés. The cliché I'm referring to here is the one that says never mix business with family or friends. I guess some of us have to learn the hard way.

Four years after the bakery closed down, my husband's friend approached him with a business proposition. His previous business partner had just retired due to ill health, and he was looking for a new challenge.

This man was as close as family to my husband – maybe closer, in some instances. They were childhood friends, he'd been best man at our wedding, and was godfather to our son. And they'd been looking for a way to work together for years. It seemed now was the perfect time.

One would think that after everything we'd been through and the experience we'd had with the bakery, we'd have learned our lesson. Sadly, I can't say that's the case. About six months into the new partnership, they called me to the offices one afternoon. They needed administrative support and wanted me to come on board as their office manager.

I agonised over the decision since the two of us would, once again, be working for the same company. We'd thought it would be different this time since we'd essentially be working for ourselves. Working toward manifesting our own dream life, instead of helping others make theirs a reality. But things aren't always as they seem to be.

We would find that out the hard way.

For four years we worked hard, building a solid reputation. The business was growing year on year, and we were starting to show a decent profit as early as year two. We knew business was good, but not good enough to support the large performance bonuses my husband was being paid by the end of year three.

Roughly halfway into year four, his health took a bit of a knock. His blood pressure was through the roof and, up until the day our house doctor died, he could never figure out how my husband never had a stroke or a heart attack because of it.

One night as we were getting ready for bed, he told me about his suspicion that something was off. What exactly, was yet to be determined, he just knew it was "something".

One afternoon it all came to a head. My husband discovered documents in the walk-in safe that made him feel devastated, betrayed, angry and a million other emotions. The details are irrelevant now, but the impact they had at the time was enormous.

For the third time, we found the dream life we'd been working so diligently for would crumble to dirt yet again. But these documents forced our hand. We had two choices – stay and potentially see everything we'd worked for taken away, not to mention the possibility of prison. Or, we could walk away and lose everything. Even more than the two previous times combined.

Since the documents made it clear that something underhanded was going on and that my husband had been set up as the fall guy, he would more than likely do jail time for being the patsy. So really, what choice did we have?

Knowing what lay ahead, walking away was the hardest thing we've ever had to do.

The Awakening
There is nothing like these times in your life that teach you who your true friends are. And the following two years certainly taught us that. But, yet again, I dug deep into the well of strength I'd discovered within myself over the previous decade of our own personal 'comedy of errors'.

Just after I started working at the property brokerage, The Secret took the world by storm. This led us to finding a book called The Jackrabbit Factor, and these books took us down a new path of discovery. It opened my eyes and mind to an entirely new – to me – world and as we journeyed down this newly discovered path, I realised a fundamental truth. My internal compass was so far off true north, I had no possible way of finding success if I continued on the same trajectory.

I was now working as a criminal court transcriptionist. Each day that I typed up the transcripts of the cases I was assigned, my soul died just a little more. I was not a naïve young girl anymore, blissfully oblivious to the horrors of the world, but I'd never been exposed to them quite like this.

I knew I wouldn't be able to do this job for too many more years before I burnt out, so I started to look around for something new. I am a qualified executive assistant with years of experience, secretarial and office administrative tasks were my forte, but the thought of returning to corporate didn't have my heart jumping for joy. The alternative to that, however, was to continue listening to the abhorrent things people did to each other and allow it to kill bits of my soul until I became a shadow of my former self. Something had to give, I just hoped it wouldn't be me.

My only reprieve from the hell of my work was my writing. In 2014, I rediscovered my love of writing and turned to it as a form of escape. A way to exorcise the ghosts of cases that had taken up residence in my head.

There are some cases so horrific that they will live with me for the rest of my life. But one such case led to me writing my debut novel. It was a form of therapy for me, a means to work through the trauma of things I'd heard.

My Biggest 'Aha' Moment

Realising I couldn't go on like this indefinitely, I began to consider my options. Finally, I settled on life coaching. I'd met an amazing woman a few years back who did this and I figured, I had nothing to lose and everything to gain.

At the beginning of each session, she would always ask me how I was doing, how the previous week had been and how my writing was going. Every week was the same. And I found the routine of it soothing. In a world of uncertainty, those three questions at the start of each coaching session brought me comfort.

I had lost my father rather suddenly just two years prior and couldn't face the idea of taking time to properly grieve his passing. So I buried my pain deep and continued with the business of living. With gentle but firm guidance, this beautiful soul helped me find the strength to honour his memory, celebrate his life, and mourn my feelings of loss. One of the many 'aha' moments she brought me during our coaching together.

But it wasn't until we'd been meeting regularly for some months that I had my biggest 'aha' moment of all.

Figuring It Out

I had always considered that my purpose for being here on planet Earth was to be of service. To my mind, the way to be of service was to become a doctor, nurse, psychologist, therapist, or something along those lines.

On this particular day, our session started the same way it always did. She asked her usual questions. How are you? How's the week been? How's the writing going? As I was sharing with her what a fabulous week of writing I'd had since we'd last spoken, she stopped me.

"Are you listening to yourself?" she asked.

"Sorry?" I replied, somewhat confused by her question.

"Are you hearing the words coming out of your mouth?" She rephrased the question.

"Well, yeah, I'm the one saying them." Still as confused as ever.

"No, my sweet friend, I don't think you are. Listening that is."

"To be honest, I'm really lost."

She laughed. "Lovely, do you have any idea how you light up when you're talking about your writing? I don't think you do. Your passion shines through so very brightly. You've been searching for something that was there all along."

"Um, I'm not sure I understand."

"Your search for purpose is right there in front of you. I've just been waiting for you to see it."

"But writing isn't being of service," I replied.

"In your opinion," She paused a moment, then continued. "You love to read, so let me ask you this. What does reading mean to you? What does it bring you?"

"Reading transports me to any number of worlds, it provides an escape from reality for a bit, it allows me to immerse myself in someone else's happy-ever-after for a little while."

"And writing? Why do you write?"

"I want to give others the same gift that reading gives to me. I want to offer them an opportunity to get lost in a world where love wins every single time."

"So then tell me how that isn't being of service? Sure, it may not be quite the linear definition of service as you understand it, but to my mind that is still being of service."

And that moment right there is when all the pieces of the puzzle shifted into a clear image. A series of seemingly complicated questions led to the simplest path to figuring my purpose out.

Listening To The Universe
Having finally figured out where my passion and path lay, I got more serious about my writing. I wrote every opportunity I got, invested time and money in learning more about the

craft and found an organisation dedicated to writing romance – my chosen genre.

As much as I was flourishing on my writing journey, the counterbalance to that was how miserable I was in my day job. More and more signs cropped up that this was not what I should be doing anymore, but I was having a hard time finding a new job. So I hung in there, dying a little more inside each day, yet too fearful to take the leap of faith due to the circumstances of the past decade that held me in a weird, unhealthy limbo.

Until the universe stepped in. Out of the blue, I received an email from the company I contracted to, thanking me for my faithful and valued service over the last four years. Due to the fact they'd lost their contract with the Department of Justice, they would be closing the company down and all the typists were being released. No retrenchment package, no notice period, just thank you and, "We wish you well in your future endeavours."

It was almost as if the universe was saying, "I've been telling you repeatedly it was time for a change, and you still aren't listening. Now I'll simply give you no option. Take that leap of faith."

As I stared at the email, all I could think was, "You have got to be kidding me. How many more times can this happen to me?" I was angry – at these people for caring so little for those of us who'd given so much of ourselves, at the universe for forcing my hand when I wasn't ready to take that leap, and the world in general.

In my mind, I saw everything that had happened as failure and never spoke of it. I was ashamed of our lack of success – to be honest, I felt like the worst kind of loser. Clearly not worthy of personal success in the business arena.

But the longer I worked with my coach, focusing on my mindset and how I viewed these traumatic experiences the more I came to some important realisations. And this is what I learned.

These 'failures' were nothing more than life experiences. The only shame they held was that with which I viewed them. They were lessons, teaching me about what I wasn't meant to be doing – in fact, it was the universe showing me just how far off my true north I was. I simply hadn't been paying attention.

What I perceived as service was my limited definition of the word. I can be of service to my readers through my words, giving to them the same gift that other authors' words bring me. However, the most important thing I learned was that I am stronger than I ever believed I was. I can endure and overcome. And now that I have found my path, my purpose, my why, I am successful because it is my heart's passion. It was always that simple, and that complicated, all along.

A Final Word

My hope in sharing this tiny snapshot of my life is that you'll come to see that we all hold that strength within us. Beyond a shadow of a doubt, I believe that if I could get through all that I have over my lifetime, anyone can.

You are a Queen, deserving of all the beauty that life holds for you. Everything you need is within you to achieve your dream life. I'm not saying it will be easy, but I am saying it will be worth it. And when you finally accept that life is indeed, happening for you and not to you that's when you awaken your magic. All that is required is a leap of faith, beyond the boundaries of your comfort zone. And I know you can do it; I believe in you.

I finally found the courage to follow my heart and now it's your turn.

About Me

I am a South African author and writing coach, living in the city of Cape Town with my husband, son, two crazy rescue dogs and a cat with plenty of cattitude.

A lifelong love affair with reading got me writing at a young age, but it wasn't until I was retrenched in 2017 that I finally found the courage to write my first book, Love at Last, leading to its publication in 2018.

I'm addicted to coffee, books and finding humour in life, not to mention happy endings against all odds.

As well as being a proud and active member of the Romance Writer's Organization of South Africa (ROSA), I am also thrilled to be a contributing author in Samantha A. Cole's Suspenseful Seduction World, Vi Keeland and Penelope Ward's Cocky Hero Club as well as Susan Stoker's Special Forces world.

To the ones who held me up and gave me strength when I couldn't find my own. Thank you for never wavering in your love and belief. I am who I am today because of you. I love you and I am eternally grateful for you.

Chloë Bisson's Top 4 Lessons On Courage

Chloë Bisson
Multiple Award-Winning Business Owner
International Speaker
Queens In Business

"Courage is contagious."– Brene Brown

On my journey of self-awareness and personal development over the years, I have often wondered what true courage is.

I used to believe that courage was the opposite of fear.

Now, if you nodded your head as you read that statement then lovely, you might need to sit down.

What I've come to realise is that courage isn't the absence of fear at all. Courage is the ability to feel fear and allow it to fuel you, not control you.

How can we learn to do this? Here, I share my top four lessons on courage to help you.

Lesson #1: You Can't Have Courage Without Fear
If courage is the act of feeling fear and pushing yourself outside of your comfort zone, then courage is only ever needed when fear is present.

If there is no fear, courage isn't needed.

My first memory of feeling courage was when I was 15 years old and I decided to stand up to my dad and disagree with something he was saying. It may not seem like a huge thing now, but at the time I was shaking inside because I had no idea how he would react. I had wanted to stand up to my dad for a while, yet the fear and uncertainty stopped me in my tracks time and time again. But one day, out of nowhere, I found the courage and I did it. We shouted, we argued and we didn't talk for a while after. Whilst it was one of the hardest things I had done at that age, I knew it was the right thing to do.

Was it as scary as I thought it would be? I would be lying if I said no!

But was it worth it? Absolutely! In the end it brought us so much closer and we are a lot stronger because of it, even 15 years later.

So in order to be more courageous, you need to get comfortable with welcoming a little fear and uncertainty into your life. Whether that's setting yourself a little challenge that gives you butterflies or taking a big step to face your fears, courage will come when you give yourself the opportunity to feel the fear.

Lesson #2: Be Brave Enough To Face The Truth
One of the most challenging aspects of feeling courage isn't actually the act of facing the fear, it's the acknowledgement of the fear in the first place. It's really normal to find it hard to

be vulnerable and society, social norms and opinions of others, among other things, can make it even harder.

But the first step of courage isn't actually taking action, it's acknowledging that it's needed and acknowledging the fear. As soon as you acknowledge a fear or challenge, you take its power away. As soon as you shine a light in a dark corner, the darkness fades.

This was exactly what I experienced when I was first diagnosed with clinical depression in 2015. When the doctor gave me my diagnosis, I was completely in denial and I hardly told anyone. I was so embarrassed that, on the outside, I was so successful, yet on the inside, I felt so broken. But I knew that in order to battle it, I needed to be brave enough to acknowledge it and face it head on, and that started by telling my friends and family. They weren't easy conversations but they were needed. Those conversations shined a light in a very dark moment of my life and the more people that found out, the more the darkness faded and the more my courage grew.

So, the moral of the story is to be brave enough to acknowledge your fears. Ask yourself:

What am I afraid of?
What fears am I shying away from?
What am I avoiding talking about right now?

We all have fears and there's no shame in it. The ability to dig deep, be vulnerable and acknowledge them, that's true courage.

Lesson #3: Make Courage A Habit
When I first started speaking in public, I used to get really, REALLY nervous. I mean, with my experience of freezing on stage at 10 years old combined with my history of anxiety and panic attacks, it's safe to say becoming an award-winning international speaker was definitely not on my bucket list.

So how did it happen?

The short answer... It didn't happen overnight!

I decided I wanted to become more confident at speaking in public so I didn't dread speaking in meetings anymore and I created what I now call a 'courageous habit'. I challenged myself to speak in public as often as I could to the point that it would become a habit. At the beginning, even the thought of doing this made me feel sick, I knew it was something I needed to do.

I started speaking at networking events, waiting for what felt like the longest time ever for each person to speak before me. I then went on to speak at some smaller events and workshops, started doing Facebook Lives and then eventually was given my first big speaking gig in London to nearly 200 women a year later.

Courage doesn't have to come in a huge wave, most of the time it actually doesn't. Courage can be like a ripple in water that starts small and over time it gets bigger and bigger.

Everything gets easier when it becomes a habit. The sooner you start practising something, the easier it gets and often the fear reduces.

So, if you have something that you really want to do, set yourself a courageous habit now. Give yourself a small challenge every day where you have to practice the act of courage.

It can be saying hello to a stranger in the street, doing a Facebook Live or anything else that may make you a little nervous. Feeling the nerves is exactly what you want because when you do the action, you will start to feel what courage feels like and most importantly, how it feels to feel the fear and overcome it.

Each day that you do your courageous habit, you're teaching your mind how it feels to be courageous and the more you do it, the stronger your ability to be courageous will be.

Lesson #4: The Most Courageous Act Is To Listen To Yourself Above Others
When I started my business, many people thought I was crazy. Asking me questions like:

"Are you sure you're really ready for that?"

"You've never run your own business, how will you get paid?"

Or my all-time favourite:

"Why don't you get a 'real job' instead?"

But I couldn't shake the voice inside of me that told me it was the right path.

Hindsight is a wonderful thing, and looking back, it's safe to say I wasn't in the best state to start a business, but I listened to my intuition and followed my gut. Five years on I've run multiple six figures businesses, won multiple awards and become a three-time, number one best-selling author. Obviously, there were ups and downs on that journey (far too many to list here!) but the point is simple.

It's ok to ask for help and it's ok to listen to advice that people give you, as long as you're also listening to yourself in the process. Every decision you make is yours to choose and it's important that you own it, as you're the person that will be living with it every day.

People come and go but your inner voice, that inner strength that is telling you to be courageous, that voice will be with you until your last breath. So, listen to it, it wants you to succeed and it's got your back.

That little voice is courage.

About Me

If there is only one thing you need to know about me, it is this – I believe that all women have what it takes to be successful female entrepreneurs and that women have the right to create their own businesses, their own income streams and their own happiness.

I'm a three-time number one best-selling author, an international speaker, multi-award winning entrepreneur and a Co-Founder of the Queens In Business Club.

As a chartered accountant at the age of twenty-one and director by the age of twenty-four, my life came to a sharp halt when I was diagnosed with severe clinical depression at the age of twenty-five. After months of growth and recovery, I knew I was meant for more than just the normal path and began my journey of entrepreneurship... little did I know how much of a journey it would really be!

Since then, I've been featured on the cover of Global Woman Magazine, spoken on stage alongside Kim Kiyosaki and have been featured on BBC, Fox, ABC, NBC, CW, London Business Magazine, Business Woman Today, Foundr and more.

Today, I run multiple six figure businesses, including a book publishing business that helps entrepreneurs to become best-selling authors, a global training organisation that teaches female entrepreneurs how to grow their businesses and a property business helping landlords to rent their properties for high returns and less hassle.

With all of my businesses, my passion and purpose is the same: to help people reach their full potential using what they already have, whether it's scaling their business, monetising their story or maximising their property.

Finding Your Life's Purpose

Andrea Symons
Ashtanga Yoga Teacher
Life Purpose Coach

"The past does not equal the future, unless you live there."
– Tony Robbins

I have loved fitness forever! Which is very odd as I absolutely hated physical education and games at school. It was always competitive sport that I hated with a passion… until we had dancing and pop-mobility at school which was a precursor to aerobics.

I loved to dance and went to various classes back in the day. I got very into Jane Fonda and her aerobics style.

But before I got to where I am today, I was working in an estate agency. I met my first husband around then, who looked like a young Michael Douglas. I was both infatuated and intimidated by his looks as well as his past.

He was eight years older than me and I was only twenty-four when we got married in January 1991. By September, I was pregnant, which he was NOT impressed with, and I miscarried on the same day that Freddie Mercury died, 24th November 1991. Four years later, I had a second miscarriage, and by the summer we had separated.

It was then that I found myself pregnant again. This time though, it was not my husband's. I had found solace in a work colleague and we began an on-off relationship that lasted a few years.

My parents had moved from my family home into a bungalow, and at that time I was living there and sleeping on a mattress on the dining room floor with all my belongings in black plastic bin bags. He was renting a room in a friend's house, so the situation was not ideal.

Even though I had miscarried twice before, I knew this was not a good time for me to have a baby. After a lot of tears, we both decided that I should have a termination. At twenty-eight, this was not what I had thought would be happening. I was a grown woman for goodness sake, previously married, not an impetuous teenager!

In writing this chapter, I went back and forth on whether I should even share this part of my story. However, I have been carrying this around with me for so long now and it's not really serving me. I did what I had to do at the time (hindsight is a great thing and after reading what comes next you might feel the same).

I also believe that as women, we must decide for ourselves what is right for us at any given moment in time. I firmly believe in 'my body, my choice'. And if you're reading this and have gone through anything similar, please do not feel guilty or shameful about your decision. You do what is right for you and not what anybody else says you should do.

During this time, I decided to renew my love of aerobics and train to teach it, qualifying in 1996 and opening a franchise for Rosemary Conley Diet and Fitness Clubs the very next year.

By 1999, I had met my second husband. I obviously like an older man, as he is 14 years older than me! He had three children of his own and had also had a vasectomy. I do pick them!

I then found out that I would need IVF to conceive – I had blocked tubes and not very well functioning ovaries. We had to have what is known as ICSI treatment, where one particular sperm is inserted directly into the egg for hopeful fertilisation.

Unfortunately, my teaching of aerobics was not really conducive to this and it was then that I discovered yoga. I went to several classes but it wasn't until I went to an Ashtanga yoga class that I eventually found my home.

Ashtanga yoga is almost like a dance. It's a set sequence of moves that is like choreography, a moving meditation. Two years later, in 2006, I qualified and have been teaching it ever since.

After four unsuccessful IVF attempts, we opted to go for egg donation. It was our only chance of conception by then. It did take me a while to accept that a donor option was the only way forward, as any baby then conceived would have none of my DNA.

However, after a lot of soul searching, I came to terms with it. Plus, any said baby would certainly have my blood as it would have been growing inside me for nine months and without me it would not have existed.

At the first attempt, I should have known better (especially now as I work a lot with intuition!). 7th July 2005. The day of the bombings in London. Everyone was trying to get out of the city while we were trying to get in for my embryo transfer. It was the most eerie feeling, like the apocalypse had occurred. Outcome – unsuccessful.

We had another two attempts with an egg donor after that. The last one being in July 2008, which unfortunately resulted in an ectopic pregnancy and emergency surgery to save my life. I decided no more. They also didn't tell me at the time that this would set me through to an early menopause!

Law Of Attraction
Throughout this time, I had used my love of yoga, the love of my Cavalier King Charles spaniels, and my belief in the law of attraction to help guide me through.

I have been determined not to become bitter over this. I could very well have become one of those people who say, "Why me?" Instead, I say, "Well, why not me?" It has taught me some very good lessons in life. I feel I am much more compassionate and empathetic to people because of it.

My yoga teaching has taught me to try to learn non-attachment to the outcome of events, to learn to accept things as they are. And law of attraction states that like attracts like, so the more positivity you put out into the universe, the more positivity comes back to you. Likewise, negativity too.

That's not to say you cannot have negative thoughts, as that would be virtually impossible. Rather, it's to not dwell on them, not get attached to them. Just acknowledge them and let them go. Easier said than done sometimes, I know!

I originally got into the law of attraction when a friend gave me a copy of The Secret to read, whilst I was going through my treatments. I immediately found it fascinating and it really resonated with me. Especially the idea that the thoughts and things that you put out into the universe can come back to you.

It's funny, I always remember my dad, who I feel has had a bit of a chip on his shoulder, always saying to me that "money attracts money, like attracts like." I think he has been intimidated by various members of our family who had money when we did not.

My dad was a typical London taxi driver and I think of him as the lovechild of Victor Meldrew and Alf Garnett! He feels hard done by in life and that life owes him. His mum passed away when he was twenty-four – before I was born – and his father then remarried. When he died not long after without having left a will, my dad got absolutely nothing from the inheritance.

My mum is my absolute hero. Her mum (my grandma) unfortunately had multiple sclerosis and I never knew her to be able to walk. Subsequently my parents had no help when I was born, and thereafter, when my brother was born.

Referring back to law of attraction, my dad had a negative attitude towards life and now, looking back I can see that that is what attracted more negativity in his life.

However, my brother and I never wanted for anything as children. We lived in a decent house, always had plenty of food and ate at the dinner table every night as a family. We were able to go on holiday, mainly to Spain every year, and my parents went on many cruises over the years. So I cannot understand how my dad could have had such a negative view, particularly towards money.

That scarcity mindset had certainly rubbed off on me and I am still working on it to this day. Although, because of my belief patterns surrounding the law of attraction, I have always found that as soon as one door closes (like losing a class or a client), I always get another one to replace it. Always.

It's like, when you are looking for a car. If you are thinking of buying a white Honda hybrid, you will all of a sudden see loads of them on the road. It's not that there are loads more on the road, it is because your brain is tuned in to see them as that is what you are focusing on. Where focus goes, energy flows.

A Magical Place
Being immersed in yoga, I loved how fit, flexible, strong and healthy it made me FEEL. After a good yoga practice, I feel like I can take on the world! And I wanted to share that with other people too. It doesn't even have to be about changing loads of people's lives. It can start with just one person.

Having a profound effect on just one person will start the ripple effect. If that one person feels good about themselves, they will then start to give out positive vibes and intentions to everyone else they encounter in their day. Thereby enhancing other people's high vibrations and good feelings too. I always remember this great quote by Maya Angelou: "People will forget what you said, people will forget what you did, but people will never forget how you made them feel."

Lockdown was hard for me with regards to my teaching. I am very much a people person, so when everything went online I really struggled. At that time I didn't have a powerful enough computer/laptop to support Zoom sessions, so I had to do it all on my phone which was very hard as I couldn't see anyone clearly enough! So as soon as we could go back to teaching face-to-face, I was there.

We started back at David Lloyd clubs in marquees outside. I love being in the warm, so being in a marquee with the 'walls' open in the freezing cold was not conducive for yoga sessions. However, just the thrill of being back with people and dressing appropriately got me through it. Now we are more or less back to normal which is great.

The one positive thing for me through lockdown was that I found time to rediscover my own personal yoga practice. Even though, for me, teaching wasn't great online, it meant I could access a lot of other classes. To put my student hat back on instead of my teacher's hat.

I was practising with the same teacher that I saw when I last went to India. He has a place in Leeds, so because I'm in Hertfordshire bordering North West London, it was great.

As I said, I met this teacher on my second visit to a fabulous yoga retreat, Purple Valley in Goa, India. The first time I went was when I turned fifty. My parents, my husband and I funded the trip for my birthday in 2016. This was the first time I had been anywhere on my own for over 20 years. I had to really step out of my comfort zone.

I had all these fears and worries going on in my head. What was I thinking – a fifty year old middle aged, middle class, menopausal, Jewish white woman, travelling all the way to

India – ON MY OWN! Would I be the oldest person there? Would I be safe? Would I like the people? Would I get ill? Would I get on with anybody? What would the accommodation be like? Would I be able to cope with all the yoga? Would I be able to cope with the heat? So I just booked for one week. A long way to go for just one week!

I decided that I wanted to get there on a direct flight instead of either changing at Dohar or Mumbai as my sense of direction is horrendous! I got a train from Watford Junction station (which is only about 10 minutes away from my house) to Manchester and caught the flight direct to Goa from there. I know it was odd, travelling north to go back south and east again, but it made me feel safe.

When I arrived, I realised I needn't have worried about anything! I definitely was not the oldest person there, the food was outstanding, the yoga was great and I loved the heat. Everyone there was lovely as we all had something in common to begin with – our love of yoga.

The accommodation was basic but clean and I definitely felt safe. In fact, so safe that I couldn't wait to go back for another visit. I totally fell head over heels in love with it and couldn't wait to return.

I went back again in November 2018. By this time, I had a client whose brother happened to live in Goa and he ran an animal sanctuary called WAG (Welfare for Animals in Goa). They do amazing work there, sterilising and neutering the street dogs and also looking after injured cows and other animals, of which there are many.

On my second visit I went for two weeks, as this time, I felt far more courageous and confident. I went to see WAG and met the people there who are just amazing.

There is something truly magical about Goa and even though I have only been there twice, it is now on my vision board to one day retire and live there permanently.

I have become truly immersed into Indian culture and I now (tongue firmly in cheek) call myself a HinJew! I watched an amazing documentary about a year or so ago called Daughters of Destiny. It chronicles the lives of five impoverished, untouchable girls attending a boarding school called Shanti Bhavan in Tamil Nadu as they strive for a better future.

This documentary inspired me so much that I wanted to make a difference to underprivileged girls. I did some research and I found a place in Goa called Mango Tree which does exactly this. I now sponsor two girls there and hopefully the next time I can go and visit Goa, I will be able to meet them. I would love to say to these girls that getting an education is so vitally important so they can get themselves out of poverty and create a better future, not just for themselves, but for their families and their communities too. I think this about all girls.

I have discovered that for me, not having children has probably been the best thing that could have ever happened to me. It has taken my life into different directions. Directions that I could never have dreamed of, had I been the typical North West London Jewish princess (nothing wrong with that if that's what you want) – but I have never been a typical Jewish princess anyway!

Finding My Strength

I have discovered a different sense of purpose in life. One that has taken me a long time to discover, but I am glad that I got here. What I truly find fulfilling is encouraging other people (women particularly) to find what their life purpose is.

It doesn't even necessarily have to be about career either. As a life purpose coach I want to encourage women to make changes in their lives that last. To quote from the text book I am learning from: "To empower, motivate and inspire people to look at their lives from a different perspective. To discover their passion and purpose. To help people bring their dreams and desires into the light."

I have dedicated nearly 26 years in the health and fitness industry to help people empower themselves and take responsibility over their bodies. To nurture themselves, feed themselves the best possible foods and to move their bodies which enables them to feel great in body, mind and spirit.

I am now dedicating the rest of my life to helping others in a different way. I'm not planning on hanging up my yoga mat any time soon, but am taking my life purpose into a different direction.

Part of the reason I came to this realisation is because of what has happened to my husband over the last seven months or so.

As I mentioned earlier, my husband is 14 years older than me. He has three beautiful grown-up daughters, and four grandchildren.

In September 2021, he was sent a stool sample kit in the post from the NHS for testing. This is a kit that is sent to people once they pass the age of 60. He duly did the test and sent it off, not giving anything a second thought.

He was then contacted as they found some abnormalities and asked if he could come in for more tests and a colonoscopy. The results were unfortunately not great. He needed further tests, CT scans, PET scans and more.

We had an appointment with the colorectal consultant who confirmed that he had bowel cancer. He was sent for further tests. Another appointment confirmed the size of the cancer which was thankfully operable, however, they also found pancreatic cancer too. When I heard this, my heart stopped and my stomach lurched.

I was aware that pancreatic cancer is one of the worst you can get and unlikely to survive. It was a blessing in disguise that they found the bowel cancer, because if they hadn't, they certainly would not have found the pancreatic cancer.

He was then sent for a course of radiotherapy to keep the bowel cancer at bay, so they could firstly treat the pancreatic cancer. During the course he was fine, it was only a day or so afterwards that the side effects took hold. He didn't know which end things were going to come out of first!

Things calmed down a little and then he was admitted to the Royal Free Hospital in London for the surgery for pancreatic cancer. He had what is called a whipple operation. They took half the pancreas and all of his spleen. I am thankful to say that the operation was a complete success and they managed to get all the cancer out. He now has a scar all the way down his belly. He also has to take lifelong antibiotics because of the splenectomy.

At the same time that this was going on, we had a litter of puppies in the house, along with our two little Cavalier King Charles spaniels. So I was to-ing and fro-ing from the hospital, taking care of the puppies and teaching my classes too!

In May 2022, my husband had his second major operation within six months for bowel cancer. Although this was done through keyhole surgery, the operation was much trickier, due to previous surgeries and scar tissue. The recovery is a lot longer too and he has ended up with a permanent colostomy bag. As of writing this, he is still recovering and in a lot of pain. Again, the operation thankfully was a success and they managed to get all the cancer out with no further treatment necessary.

Sometimes it can take major events to happen in your life before you start to question, what am I here for? What is my life's purpose? Why do I do what I do? Who is it for? Who am I serving? What is MY why?

So this course literally fell into my lap one day after visiting my husband in hospital. I thought, YES, this is exactly what I am looking for. This is now my life purpose, to help you find your life purpose.

This also happened because I believe in keeping an open mind about things, listening to what messages are being sent to me from the universe, listening to my intuition, and believing in the law of attraction. Having an attitude of gratitude is key.

I am so grateful for the challenges I have had in my life. I believe that you are given what you can handle, and as the old saying goes, what doesn't kill you, makes you stronger.

I feel stronger now at nearly 56 than I have ever felt in my life before.

My advice is to listen to your gut instinct – it is barely ever wrong. Listen to your intuition, keep an open mind, be grateful for everything you have in life. It doesn't matter if it takes you a while to find your purpose, as everything you are doing is guiding you in the right direction.

About Me

I am an Ashtanga yoga teacher and soon to be life purpose coach to help people to find their mission and to enable me to do public speaking on the subject.

I see myself as a guide. To inspire, motivate and empower you to find your own way in life, to find YOUR life's purpose.

I have been in the health and fitness industry for nearly 26 years and a perineal student, having also studied EFT, fertility yoga, nutrition, face yoga, law of attraction, mindfulness, life coaching and mindful nutrition, among other qualifications.

I am passionate about helping people become the best version of themselves by creating a positive mindset and having a lot of fun and laughter along the way.

I have been interested in self-development for the last decade or so, and am now starting to incorporate it more and more into my professional career. Last year, I also completed the Tony Robbins Unleash the Power Within virtual event, which was extraordinary. I learned so much from this and had many breakthrough and 'aha' moments.

I believe we continue to grow through learning and our beliefs can either empower us or keep us stagnated. A belief is just a thought that we have attached meaning to. Change your thoughts, change your beliefs.

My other passion is dogs, particularly Cavalier King Charles spaniels. We have two at the moment, and in the past have had three others too! We have bred litters from them over the years. This is such a life affirming thing to do, so rewarding but utterly hard work!

I am so very grateful to the Queens In Business Club for this opportunity to collaborate in writing this book and I look forward to the many more opportunities to come my way and doors that it will open. Trust the timing. Timing is everything – and this is MY time and YOURS too.

"Celebrate the *genius* of who you are openly"

Tanya Grant
The Branding Queen

You Have Everything To Give

Tracey King
Founder and Director
Sensory Play UK

"It may be necessary to encounter the defeats, so you can know who you are, what you can rise from, how you can still come out of it." – Maya Angelou

Trigger Warning[1]

It was the school holidays and we had planned to have a drive to the seaside, but the heavens opened and plans needed to be changed. To cut a long story short, my husband wanted to do one thing and my boys and I wanted to go to the cinema, which we did after dinner (lunch for readers down south).

One argument led to another, which was a regular occurrence, but this day I will remember forever, because this is the day that something inside me snapped.

In the cinema foyer, my husband was in my face telling me that I was selfish. I chose the cinema rather than swimming, I chose McDonald's rather than KFC, I chose Marley and Me rather than whatever else was showing that day and so on and so on. And I am still so proud of myself for allowing the next few words to leave my mouth. "You think I'm selfish, well I'll show you selfish!" I was trembling inside, not with

---

[1] Suicidal ideation and domestic violence

fear, but because I knew this was the moment my life would change forever – for the better!

The Battles

I want to rewind my story for a moment, to give you an idea of what life was like from childhood. I was just one year old when my parents were told that my older brother, Scott, had epilepsy and brain damage, which I can only imagine would have been a massive shock and confusing time for them. By the age of three, my parents had divorced and I suddenly found myself living in a single parent family in a council home with a brother with additional needs.

I went through the next eight years or so feeling ripped in two. My dad demanding to be able to take me to his place on weekends and my mum refusing to let me go because he was five minutes late picking me up. I sometimes wonder if they ever realised that I was watching them through the gap in the kitchen door as they were screaming at each other, Mum repeatedly hitting Dad, and Dad trying to get away from her. Then Dad coming into the hall where I had been standing, crying, telling me to put my coat and shoes on because we were leaving, while blood was appearing from a large cut on his forehead. My brother stayed at a residential 'special' school in Cheshire, so he rarely had to witness these types of scenes.

As the years went by, mum suffered badly with depression and was often in and out of mental health hospitals. I remember occasions when she rang school and told them to send me home (my school was literally a three minute walk from my house). When I arrived home, she was on the phone to the Samaritans and handed the phone to me.

"Tracey, your mum is feeling very sad at the moment and she needs your help. I need you to find all her tablets and hide them so that she can't get to them, you'll be saving her life by doing this."

I remember a couple of separate incidents where she 'passed out' and I had to get help. I say it in speech marks because to this day I still believe that she was faking it to get attention. I could be wrong, but that's my personal opinion.

Mum would get angry very easily over the littlest of things and was very strict in the sense that I could not bring my toys downstairs. Very rarely was I allowed to play in my bedroom with my toys. She did allow me, however, to sweep the bits up in the kitchen when the hoover was broken and she also allowed me to dust the skirting boards on the staircase, although that might only have been a one-off after I came rolling down from the top step to the bottom.

Whenever my friends came to see if I was playing out, Mum would always say I was busy helping her. The only time I can really recall me being allowed outside was when Scott was home from school during the holidays and Mum wanted me to make sure he stayed safe. He had a ride-along car which he often would drive round the back of the house to where a row of garages were, and guaranteed, there would always be one left open, which Scott would drive the car into and I would always be the one getting told off by the owner of the garage.

The most heart-breaking time I remember is the day my brother and I were arguing over a cup we both wanted to use. Scott was unable to speak full sentences but that didn't stop him shouting at me and pulling my hair from its roots. We were both trying to get hold of this particular cup but we both lost the grip and the cup smashed into pieces. My mum completely lost it. I'd seen her angry many times over, but nothing like this. She repeatedly hit my brother over the head. The words she was screaming were inaudible. Even to this day my heart breaks as I picture my brother cowering while Mum just hit and hit and hit. All I remember is screaming for help... Surely someone could hear and rescue us from this maniac of a woman? The rest of that memory is blank. Obviously, and thankfully, that event did not end in tragedy.

At school I was certainly not a confident child and I very much believed that everyone else was so much better than me. I was not academically bright, and I hated sports or anything where we had to participate in groups. I often got bullied (mainly by the boys).

On one occasion when I was around nine years old, I can recall walking with a friend through the playground at the end of the school day. I had briefly looked back to see who was behind us and the next thing I knew, these lads who were a few years older than me, pinned me down and began kneeing me in the face. My friend ran to get his mum and by the time she got to me, the group of boys ran off and I was laying there with blood all down my face. The punishment for the boys was the cane and slipper.

There was another episode where another boy said he was going to 'bray' me the next day, all because a chair that was placed on top of a table fell on him and I giggled along with the rest of the class. The next morning, as I was heading to school, this boy spotted me and chased after me. I ran out of the school grounds and found somewhere to hide. I was too scared to go back to school and too scared to go home.

At this time, my dad had a flat almost behind my mum's house, so I headed there. Unfortunately, he was at work, so I went to his neighbour and asked if I could use her phone to ring my dad. He had to get his boss to drive him home, then he took me back to my mum's. The police were there, and they were not sympathetic and just reminded me that I'd made everyone worry about me, then my mum took me back to school. I don't recall much of the conversation in the headteacher's office, other than telling her about why I ran away, but what I do recall is the quote she reeled off to me which still makes me shudder to this day. "Sticks and stones may break my bones, but words will never hurt me." What a load of codswallop!

Downward Spiral

Fast forward three years. I still hated life. My mum was still in and out of mental health hospitals and I was shipped from pillar to post. I was now at high school and still had no confidence and my self-esteem was shockingly low. The only thing I was happy about was that I was now attending an all-girls school, so I no longer had to deal with those vicious boys!

During an episode of my mum being in hospital, I'd had enough. I had taken my cousin and best friend to my mum's house and while they were entertaining each other, I was in the next room with a bottle of my mum's tablets. I have little recollection of my cousin practically dragging me to his house. Apparently, I looked very drunk and foaming at the mouth. It turns out I had taken my mum's sleeping pills, so thankfully, no lasting damage – although I still do like to sleep a lot! The only thing that came from that moment was that I got to live with my dad. No one ever considered that an eleven-year-old might also be dealing with depression. The whole incident was just swept under the carpet.

By now, I'd gone through a variety of nicknames including the usual, 'fatty'. In high school, I'd become known as 'sweaty Betty' (Betty had been shortened from my maiden name of Bedford, and I'm sure I don't need to explain why I was called sweaty!).

Although I felt inferior to my peers, I would still try and fit in somehow, which included smoking and bunking off school. It wasn't long before I was on the cider and sniffing poppers (or nail polish remover), whatever was available at the time, to give that moment of feeling high. In all honesty, from here on in, life became a downward spiral, but I did not know it.

My dad met his future wife and I suddenly accumulated three stepbrothers. I was going through all the usual teenage hormone issues and trying desperately to figure out life, but with little success. Eventually, after many more arguments, I ran away to London where the one positive was getting to meet my idol, Jason Donovan. I was placed in a runaway home for three weeks and it was there that I found out that when I was younger, I had been placed on the at-risk register. I then moved into my auntie's home for a few months (I will forever be grateful to her for putting up with all my crap), then moved back to my mum's to try and rebuild our relationship. Unsuccessfully I might add.

By the age of sixteen, I had moved into a hostel for young people, met my future husband, fallen pregnant three months later, and became a mum at the age of seventeen.

Out of respect for my sons, my in-laws, and even my ex-husband, I'm not going to go into details of my marriage, but I will at this point apologise to my boys for everything they had to put up with, listen to, and witness throughout their childhood.

I hated my childhood and always wanted to ensure that my kids would have a better time growing up. That is something I failed at miserably, but I am so grateful that they have turned into the most amazing young men who have finally broken the cycle, and I know they will treat their partners with the utmost respect and kindness so that their children will grow up in a more loving environment.

118

During my early adulthood, having two little boys while still being a teenager was certainly no easy ride. There was very little support at that time for young mums and I remember living off income support, which was very low for people under the age of nineteen.

The Social never took into consideration those who had their own house with the same bills to pay as people over the age of nineteen. I was easy prey to the loan sharks (to me, even companies like Provident and Greenwoods are as bad as the nasty loan sharks). I soon got into debt, and to this day I am still living with the effects and consequences of the choices made back in 1993.

I was still enjoying having many drinking sessions with mates and I'd often be found behind the microphone on karaoke nights at the local pub. Over the next 15 years, life was still very up and down. I had very low self-esteem, although many would not believe that because to them, I would come across as a confident person. One thing I believe I was very good at was wearing the mask. It's amazing the amount of things I could fake! I even got to the stage where I could fake being sober.

Drinking certainly had become a major part of my life, and I think it definitely got worse after my mum died in 2005, six months after she'd had gastric bypass surgery. She lost double the weight she was supposed to lose, going from 30 to 15 stone. Her organs were slowly shutting down, and I had to make the decision whether or not to have her put on a dialysis machine, which may or may not have bought her a smidge of time.

My relationship with my mum never really improved, I think we just tolerated each other more, and she did do her best to be a good grandma. But now I was faced with her life in my hands. I can't even begin to describe what was going through my head at the time, but I will admit that some of my thoughts weren't good thoughts. After umpteen trips outside for cigarettes, while all my aunties and uncles were by her bedside, I finally told the doctor to let her go.

The one thing that still sticks in my mind about that cold November night is trying to stop her ripping her oxygen mask off and her lashing out, leaving a nasty scratch on my hand. It took me straight back to the moment she got angry with me when I was seven years old, and she grabbed me by my dress and scratched my chest. What a memory to end with while watching her take her last breath.

By now, cider had turned to vodka, of which I was managing to drink a litre of each day. I would take the boys to school in the morning and do my crossing patrol job. I'd then head off to my local shop and buy a small bottle of vodka. I'd drink that from 9:30am till 11:00am, then head back to school to do my job as lunchtime supervisor.

After lunch, I would head back to the shop for another small bottle of vodka. Drink that from 1:30pm till 2:30pm, then head back to school to do the school crossing again. My mother-in-law would often pick me and the boys up after school and she would comment that she could smell alcohol. Luckily for me, we would just be passing the local pub as she'd make this statement, so I would always blame that. My husband, not realising what I had already drunk in the day, would then buy me a bottle of vodka on his way home from work because he knew I was partial to a drink in the evening. This routine went on for a good three years, if not longer.

Not long after my mum had died, I think I did go through a bout of depression, but at the time, I was not aware of this. Even when I had decided I couldn't go on anymore and planned to end my life on Christmas Eve 2005.

I made arrangements for a couple of friends from church to come over for dinner. I wanted friends who believed in God to be there when my family received the news that I'd been found dead. I then told my family that I had a few more Christmas presents to buy in Leeds, and off I went.

The first place I found myself was at my mum's flat, which obviously, was no longer hers. No one had moved in yet, so I was able to peer through the window at the emptiness of the flat. I felt empty too.

I walked up the road to a nearby motorway bridge, stood staring down at the cars and contemplated jumping. Thankfully, despite my head being numb, my heart still reminded me that if I jumped, then I would cause carnage for the motorists down there, and the emergency response team too. So, I just walked.

I walked to a place called Drighlington where my dad used to take me when the fairground came to town, then got a bus to Leeds. I certainly had no real plans of buying any more presents and so for the rest of that journey I had to decide what I was going to do to end my life.

While on the bus, I wrote goodbye letters to my boys. Once I arrived in the city, I went to a shop and bought a couple of packs of paracetamol. My new plan was to get on another bus, sit at the back, and take the painkillers. Although I couldn't identify where the pain was in my body, I just needed to kill it.

I took the pills, but nothing happened. My husband by this point had been phoning and texting me, wondering where the heck I'd got to. Obviously, I had ignored all of these, but the next thing I knew, the bus that I was on had arrived at the town near where I lived. I got off, and for some reason I just started walking towards home. I was like a zombie for the next month until the day I found out I was pregnant.

Everything To Give
I was ecstatic because I'd really wanted another baby for years. I stopped drinking. Life seemed to be on the up.

And then I collapsed in agony.

It turns out it was ectopic. On 15th February 2006, I was rushed to surgery. My fallopian tube ruptured and apparently, I was lucky to be alive. And guess what, the drinking started again.

That continued until the day I decided to be selfish. Enough was enough! I did not want to continue living the life I was living. Yes, drinking and getting paralytic night after night was me being selfish, but everything else in life I did, I did for everyone else. The fact that my husband called me selfish was enough for me to see red. Life was over as I knew it.

Once I'd gone through all the drama and mental breakdowns, I finally had the courage to end the marriage and begin the life that had been waiting for me. I enrolled in college to get the childcare qualification I'd always yearned for. I began working in a nursery, discovered that my life's purpose was to help children with additional needs to have the best life they could possibly have, and the list goes on.

Because I finally had the courage to put me, my mind, my health and my future first, I was able to achieve things I never in a million years would have thought I could do. I have recently achieved, at the age of forty-five, a bachelor's degree in special educational needs and I'm about to study for a master's degree in Autism as I feel that is what I want to specialise in. I have even stood as an independent councilor candidate in my local area, and although I did not win, I am so so proud of myself for getting just under 300 votes – I even got more votes than the Liberal Democrats!

I have tried and failed in different ventures, but I am always mindful of what the word FAIL means – First Attempt At Learning. That is so true, because after all the lessons I have learned, I am now Founder and Director of Sensory Play UK and have venues throughout West Yorkshire. I am a life mentor and relax kids coach, helping children to realise that they are worth so much more than they think. I also co-own an events company with my son called ABC Connect LTD and have recently set up Event Nannies UK, providing childcare for weddings and other events.

I know that there are many women out there who feel that they have nothing to give in this world, but I want to tell you right now that you have everything to give. Your past may be the most horrific memory you have but you need to use that to help others.

This is what I am doing now, and do you know what? I am selfish, because helping others to become the best version of themselves makes me feel incredibly awesome. I have used my courage to tell my story so that other women know that they can be fiercely confident too, no matter what they have been through.

Don't stop believing in you.

About Me

I am a mum to two amazing, strong-willed sons, and a nanna to two absolutely gorgeous grandchildren. I love travelling the UK and enjoy spending tranquil moments at my static caravan in Cleethorpes.

I am obsessed with family history and have recently discovered that Walt Disney and Abraham Lincoln are (very) distant cousins of mine. Now I know where I got my passion for writing children's stories and making changes in my community from!

I run a franchise called Relax Kids Kirklees. This is where my real passion lies, in helping children understand the emotions they feel, and how they can learn techniques in dealing with anxiety. My goal is to ensure that as many children as possible know that they are amazing and that they can achieve anything they set their mind to, no matter what the haters may say.

I do admit that I have my fingers in many pies as I have so many ideas running around in my head. The most recent business that I have set up is Sensory Play UK where families can come and have some tranquil and calming time, exploring the sensory equipment. I also co-own ABC Connect LTD with my son where we supply equipment for events, this includes our sister company Event Nannies UK. Alongside all of this, I am a life mentor, specialising in mentoring people with additional needs to be more assertive and active in their communities. And in my spare time, I do the odd TV work such as Emmerdale as a supporting artist (extra).

I would like to dedicate this chapter first and foremost to my sons, Kieran and Liam. You've had to put up with a hell of a lot from me over the years. I just hope I am a better example now to you both. Also, to Lucy and Kayleigh, thank you for being such beautiful souls. I look forward to the day I can call you daughters-in-law.

A special mention to my grandchildren, Isabella and Theodore. As you grow, you will come across many obstacles that will try and stop you living your dream, but please remember that you are in control of your life and Nanna T will help you all the way to living your best life!

Practise Courage With Sunna Coleman

Sunna Coleman
Content Marketing Coach
Bloggers Inspired

"Courage doesn't always roar. Sometimes courage is the little voice at the end of the day that says I'll try again tomorrow."
– Mary Anne Radmacher

When people think of courage, they typically imagine big bold moves and a willingness to take risks. But courage isn't always so obvious.

Sometimes, courage is the ability to stay still, or persevere, or hold on.

For me, it's all about knowing yourself and what is right for you at that moment – and then having the courage to stand up for it, no matter the societal or internal pressures.

But making courageous decisions is not easy. Sometimes all we want to do is give in and settle back into a place where we feel most comfortable. What happens then? We don't grow. We don't learn. We don't inspire.

If you're reading this book, chances are you've got an insatiable entrepreneurial spirit and a drive for making real change. If that's you, courage is something you desire to maintain in order to help you fulfil your mission.

So how can we encourage more courage?

In this guide, discover helpful tips and practical advice to build a courageous attitude and keep your momentum flowing.

The Courageous Mind

As with many areas of life, courage starts with a healthy mindset. Here are two ways to nurture your mindset to help you bring out your most courageous self.

#1 Embrace Failure

In the face of failure, it is completely normal and okay to have negative thoughts. It's what you do with those thoughts afterwards that really matters. If we let our negative thoughts fester, they seep deeper into our subconscious, and affect our behaviour in the future. That means, when a new hurdle comes our way, we're likely to approach it with limiting beliefs already standing in the way of our success and blocking us from achieving our full potential.

Instead, if we embrace failure and accept that it is inevitable from time to time, we realise that it is just a part of life, rather than something we must avoid at all costs. Without failure, we never learn. Without learning, we never improve. Failure is, in fact, a necessary experience.

When we take the pressure off, we allow ourselves the freedom to face difficult situations with a strong mindset, leading to a better chance of success. Not only that, but if we do end up 'failing', we don't crumble and sabotage our future success. We see it as an opportunity for growth, gearing us up to try again.

So next time you feel like you have 'failed', ask yourself: what can I learn from this? Then, use it as ammunition to try again or adapt your strategy.

#2 Focus On Your 'Why'

Sometimes, shifting our perspective away from our own selves and onto what drives us can be the best way to keep us moving forward with courage. Whether it's your son, daughter, partner, mother, friend or the lives you want to improve in the world, remembering who or what you stand for can reignite the fire.

Because we're not just here for our own selfish reasons, we have a responsibility to do what's right – and often what's difficult – to make a positive difference to those who need, and could benefit from, our help.

Who or what do you stand for?

I stand for... _____

_____

_____

Courage-Building Habits

As well as our thoughts, our actions can be instrumental in helping us take on life with more courage. Try these three courage-building habits next time you feel yourself slipping back into your comfort zone.

#1 Resolve Uncertainty

Our biggest challenges have the potential to be our largest growth moments, but they often come with an element of fear attached. Our natural instinct, if we have the option to choose it, is to retreat back to safety. Because being brave and heading into uncertainty comes with great risk. We don't know how the situation may pan out, and that can be an uncomfortable feeling. After all, it's far easier to stick with what you know.

We all do it. Think of something in your life that you have been avoiding for a while now, but still, you toy with the idea of it every now and then. You imagine another you, in a parallel universe, who doesn't care about the consequences and just goes for what her heart desires. But the real you can't afford that luxury. You have bills to pay, a family to feed, and the potential judgement from those you are close to. Whatever it is, your fear of uncertainty in how this may unfold is holding you back. Yet, you keep coming back to this one idea. Because deep down, you want to take on that challenge.

So instead of letting uncertainty push you away from exciting opportunities, try to understand it by breaking down the varying outcomes that could occur, and reflecting over how you would handle each situation.

1. Start with considering: what's the worst that could happen? Think about the worst case scenario and

write that down. Next, think about what you can do in that situation or how you can reframe how you think about that situation to make it less of a negative experience. In other words, what would be your solution in this instance?

2. Next, think about: what's the best that can happen? Write it down and think about how you would feel in this situation and what it will do for you.

3. Once you have the answers to your worst and best case scenarios, you know that you will be able to handle everything in between!

This exercise can help relieve feelings of anxiety surrounding the unknown, helping you feel more courageous in the face of uncertainty.

#2 Practise Vulnerability
For a more fulfilled life, we need to be able to make courageous decisions – decisions that are right for us but that may not necessarily align with the opinions of others. In order to achieve this, we have to be able to let go of what other people may think. We have to become comfortable with vulnerability.

In this modern age, where sharing perfect versions of ourselves online is the norm, this has become more and more difficult. Not only do we have our close circle's opinions to consider, but those of our online audience. The thought of being subject to ridicule or judgement from keyboard warriors is enough to scare most of us into hiding any part of us that doesn't fit into the 'norm'.

But if we're all forced to look, act and think the same, we create an unrealistic version of society, where the majority feel pressured into pretending to be someone they're not. The more people that portray themselves inauthentically, the worse that the problem gets. It's how tragedies surrounding things like racism and sexism continue to exist. This is why it is vital to practise vulnerability. To open up our most authentic selves and stand up for what we believe in, not only for ourselves, but to lend our courage to others so that they can do the same.

Start small by sharing something vulnerable with a close friend. See how that feels. Then, work your way up by practising being more open and honest about how you feel with others. Not everyone will agree with what you say or think, but the point is to let go of that inevitability or comparison complex. The world is made up of diverse opinions. It's what makes us all so interesting and unique.

Eventually, with time, it will feel natural and more comfortable to let your authenticity shine. And you'll be surprised at how many others who agree with your thinking will gravitate towards you.

Colour in the heart on your favourite affirmation on the next page and use it as a daily reminder to help you practise vulnerability...

♡ Do what the ordinary fear	♡ Don't trade authenticity for approval	♡ Who I am matters
♡ Respect your voice	♡ Do what is right, not what is easy	♡ Be fearlessly you

#3 Keep Reminders

One of the best ways to convince ourselves that yes, we can do this, is by looking at our past experiences. Keeping a record of uplifting reminders that demonstrate the challenges we have overcome before, helps us to remember that we have what it takes to get through more.

Try it now, write down three times you have overcome something with courage in your life:

1. _____
2. _____
3. _____

For a bonus boost of confidence, write down how you are feeling before you take on a new challenge that requires you to be courageous. Then, once you have completed it, reflect on how you feel now. Was it as difficult as you were expecting? What helped you persevere? How do you feel about taking on new challenges now?

Keeping reminders and actively reflecting on your behaviour is a constant courage builder that helps you become your own cheerleader.

You've already got what it takes. You just need to learn to let your inner fire free.

About Me

I am an award-winning content marketing specialist, multiple international best-selling author, Chief Editor of the QIB book series, and Founder of Bloggers Inspired, helping small business owners escape social media overwhelm and take back control so that they can stand out from their competitors, attract higher quality leads and convert more sales in their business.

I could not have achieved any of this without really stepping into my courage.

After moving away from a diverse area of London to a predominantly White area as a young girl, I went from a confident child to a shy and reserved shell of myself. I experienced prejudice, stereotyping and bullies for the first time and this forced me to 'Westernise' my behaviour in order to fit in.

Years of trying to blend in soon became my norm, and by the time I realised that this was unjust, it was deeply ingrained into my personality. Breaking free of that took a lot of work. And it was scary.

But with each moment that I embraced who I am and what I believe in, my courage grew and it helped me reach higher than I ever thought I could.

Courage takes consistency and time. I still work on it today. I feared public speaking for so long but it's the next hurdle I am tackling with courage by my side. Since venturing into this unknown space, I have spoken on multiple stages, alongside representatives from the likes of the BBC, ITV, C4, CNN, Disney and Warner Brothers.

Courage can help you achieve incredible things. And I hope my courage can help someone else feel ready to harness theirs.

I dedicate this chapter to my mother, or 'Ami' as we call her in Urdu. Your unrelenting strength continues to inspire me. Thank you for always being fiercely courageous to protect what you love and believe in.

Follow Your Heart And Soul

Leisa Quagliata
Transformational Healing Practitioner
Strategic Intervention Life Coach
Connected To Soul

"We are stronger, gentler, more resilient, and more beautiful than any of us imagine."– Mark Nepo

Over the years I've tried my hand at many things on the never-ending quest to find out what my purpose in this lifetime is supposed to be. I travelled the world while working two jobs most of the time to pay for my first love – travel. I didn't care what I did, so long as it involved working with people and being trusted to do my own work. I should have seen the obvious signs that I would eventually become my own boss.

I remember many psychic readings in my twenties telling me I would one day own my own business but the biggest thing that stopped me was fear. I thought they were all just pulling my leg. Seriously, me, the girl who quite frequently quit a job after a few months because I was bored. How in the world would I ever be able to have my own business, when I couldn't even work out what I wanted to do long enough to stay in a job?

But that's the thing about psychic readings, they plant a seed in your mind, and without any resistant thought to block the manifestation that seed starts to grow deep down inside you, without you even knowing it.

There I was, flitting around the world, moving from country to country, job to job. If it didn't fit into my backpack, it didn't come with me to the next destination. Life was carefree, fun and exciting. But one thing was missing and that was love. I watched as everyone around me eventually paired up with partners and either headed home or applied for spousal visas to remain in the country of their now foreign-born partner.

Eventually, love did find me, and two children later, I thought I had it all. The nice house, husband, two gorgeous kids, financial security and even a new car. Life was sweet and I could hardly believe that I had been so lucky to meet such an amazing partner.

But then one day, without warning, my whole life came crashing down around me when my husband came home and declared, "I don't think I can stay married to you any longer." WTF? Where had this come from? I mean, I know it had been tough since the boys were born, but that's what happens when kids come along. You just assume it will get better the older they get.

His reasons? He wanted more children and I didn't. That was it, end of discussion. There I was, thirty-six years of age, holding two toddlers with no clue what to do next. In a daze, I took myself up to my bedroom, sat on the side of the bed and cried so hard I thought my heart would burst.

Still in shock, I thought about who to call first. I knew once I rang my parents, there would be no coming back from admitting that my marriage had failed and I too had failed. I decided to ring my best friend and was a little surprised to hear myself say, "Well, at least I get a second chance to be happy", followed by, "I better go back and get that degree I quit 20 years ago."

The decision to go to university had nothing to do with a desire to further my education and everything to do with survival. I just knew that if I was ever going to be able to give my kids a life that they deserved, I would have to get a degree and break the financial ceiling I had set for myself when working administration jobs.

University was a welcome distraction from the chaos that had become my life and somehow, I managed to breeze through my degree in just under two and a half years, only to land my first job after uni as an administration officer for a financial adviser's office.

Yep, two and a half years and $20,000 debt later, I ended up right back where I started – except this time, I was earning fifty per cent less than what I was earning before I went to university. I had to laugh at the irony. It would be years later, after I learned about unconscious fears and subconscious money blocks, that I would understand how this had manifested into my existence.

Taking The Leap

Within 18 months, I was a fully-fledged financial adviser, but my boss had an expectation that I would source my own clients. With this in mind, I thought to myself, "If I'm going to build a business and a brand, it's going to be my own."

For the next seven months, I squirreled away as much money as I could with the goal of starting my own business. At the time, I was only earning $22,000 plus whatever government assistance I could secure, so there was not a lot left over to save. But that's the thing about motivation and desire, when the chips are down, that's when I seem to work the hardest towards what I want. I kept telling myself that failure is not an option.

In July 2015, I had coffee with my boss and told him I was going self-employed. He was fully supportive and a big help in those early days. With no real client base, I knew things would be tough. I made my first rookie mistake when I thought all I really had to do was replace my measly part-time income which at that stage was only $25,000. How wrong I was.

I had not fully understood that it was not just my income I had to replace, but all the expenses my boss had been paying for. You know, rent, electricity, software, licensee fees, the list goes on. In fact, the list of expenses started at $30,000 and that was before I even paid myself.

For the next 12 months, I diligently built my client base through a combination of networking and marketing. Having been through my own hellish divorce and starting over from scratch, I had a passion for (and tons of experience) in helping women rebuild and better protect themselves financially now and in the future.

I began writing and delivering my own financial education seminars, using the seminars as lead magnets to get prospective clients in the door. I must have been doing something right because the conversion rate of attendees to clients from my very first seminar was thirty percent.

I was on a roll, the momentum had begun and by the end of that first year, I had a steady income stream that seemed to be paying the bills, putting food on the table and keeping a roof over my head, even if it wasn't paying me very much in the way of supporting a lifestyle barely above the poverty line.

As my seminars became more and more popular, I began attracting women who were seeking help going through their marriage breakdowns. I found myself unofficially coaching these women after hours, which identified to me a gap in the market that was desperate to be filled and that was financial divorce coaching. Knowing my current financial services licensee would never be on board with this kind of work, I began researching alternative licensees who would.

After months of due diligence and research, I felt ready to take that leap and move licensees.

Getting On With It

By 2017 – after overcoming a major financial and technical hurdle during the licensee move – I had settled into my own premises and launched my second business venture, The Financial Divorce Chick, specialising in mediating couples through a divorce. The philosophy of this business was to reduce the financial and emotional impact of divorce by helping couples focus on what they needed to restart their lives, rather than what they felt they were entitled to.

In 2018, in order to diversify into more generalised money and personal coaching, I created the LeisaQ Life-Stylist brand which continues today. Ideas for new seminars, workshops and courses flowed with ease and the results after each event were always positive and financially successful. Life was good...

Then the next major hurdle reared its ugly head. In February 2019, an unprecedented weather event considered a 'one-in-1000 year event' hit Townsville. In the short space of seven days, the Ross River Dam received 850,000 megalitres of rainfall. Businesses were wiped out, entire suburbs completely submerged under water, not to mention days, weeks and months of clean up.

Thankfully our office only suffered minor water damage, but the real effects were felt in the forced office closure and cancelled appointments. Being a business that only receives revenue once per month, these cancellations had a knock-on effect for months.

Despite the financial blow to my bank account, it was during this time I signed up for personal coaching. The cost was way out of my budget but my intuition was strongly pushing me in this direction. For once I decided to ignore my logical thinking brain and just go with my gut.

It altered the course of my life, which I believe kick-started me to where I am today. Looking back, I still have no idea how I even paid for all those coaching sessions, but I held strong in my belief, trusting that this was all going to work out in the end.

It was the year I was ostracised from my social group, lost long-term friendships and had my child support wiped out in its entirety – again. Each time I felt like giving up, I would dig deeper, double down and increase my courage and determination to prove to everyone that I could be a success. You know the old saying: "fake it until you make it". Well, that is what I felt I was doing throughout 2019. But if I thought that year was hard, it truly was just a warm up for what 2020 had in store for me.

2019 hadn't been all that bad. I did make a lot of progress. My money coaching programs were now being delivered in person and online. Client results were outstanding. Attendance at our seminars continued to grow and the financial planning side of my business continued to go from strength to strength despite new government regulations which resulted in halving our commissions and doubling our costs. By the end of the year, I had been invited to present to a few of the local private schools, which continued into the beginning of 2020. And we all know what happened next.

When Tragedy Strikes Twice

In 2020, when the Covid-19 global pandemic hit, I don't think anyone could have foreseen just how much it was going to impact our families, businesses, and our quality of life on such a grand scale. In those first few days when panic, fear and uncertainty were gripping people around the world, it was clear no one was going to be immune to the wide-reaching effects of this new and menacing disease.

As nations around the world began widespread lockdowns and global markets plummeted, I had no idea that watching my clients' share portfolios lose value was going to be the least of my problems.

In fact, it only took 15 days after Australia announced its very first lockdown for Covid-19 to become insignificant in what was about to play out in my personal life.

On Monday 6th April 2020 at 8pm, I received a phone call from my mum that would send my life careening down a path I had hoped to never visit ever again.

As I listened on the phone, my legs suddenly gave way beneath me as she told me that my younger brother had chosen to take his life a few short hours ago. In total shock, I was transported back in time to 1992 when I received a similar phone call, one that, looking back, completely altered the course of my life.

Have you ever watched that scene from the Matrix where the analyst slows down time in order to prevent Neo from talking to Trinity? As I stood there listening to Mum on the other end of the phone, suddenly I felt like time had slowed down, her voice a muffled noise in the distance. Inside my head I could hear myself screaming, "Not again!"

You see, 28 years beforehand, my mum had called to tell me my older brother had just been in a serious motorcycle accident. In shock and feeling dazed on the way to the hospital, I remember repeating to myself over and over, "Please God, let him be okay." An hour after that phone call, I found myself standing over my brother's now lifeless body thinking to myself, "Why did this have to happen?"

Those words uttered to myself all those years ago now felt like they were on repeat in my head. Had my parents not endured enough suffering over the years.

In the cold light of morning, it started to dawn on me just how quickly I felt my life had turned to sh*t. Six short weeks beforehand, I had signed five new clients, the stock market was flying high, 2020 had started with a bang and now it felt like a complete bust.

As a solopreneur, I've always loved the ability to do my own thing, make my own rules and live the work balance I desire.

However, the flipside to that is, when the chips are down, you find yourself sitting there feeling lost and alone, scrambling to work out who is there to help. Factor in my longstanding history of not knowing how to reach out and ask for help and you have a great big mess on the floor, simultaneously feeling sorry for myself and getting angry that there was no Prince Charming around to come and rescue me.

I've faced struggles in the past, but this was going to require digging deeper than anything I'd ever attempted before.

Rock Bottom
In the months that followed, I found myself actively wanting to hit rock bottom.

I'd somehow managed to hang onto all my clients, new and old, my sanity (barely) and ironically (considering I felt like I was barely working), the money continued to roll in. This was the first time I truly realised what an amazing business I had built over the years and that I was proud of my accomplishments.

But it was not all roses and sunshine. Despite appearing to be highly functioning on the outside, on the inside, I felt like I was dying, a fraud, someone wearing a mask so that the world wouldn't see the pain that had gripped my heart like a physical vice.

I knew this was a result of trying to grieve on top of unresolved grief, so I pulled out all the spiritual practices I had learned over the years and actively willed myself to hit rock bottom. I did this because I knew if I could hit rock bottom, there was only one way to go from there. I vowed to myself that I was never, ever going to find myself at the bottom again, so I better get it right this time.

My journey led me down a path where just nine months later, I would find myself making the decision to sell my financial planning practice and radically change the direction of my career.

Oh boy, when you make radical decisions when highly emotive, you better strap in tight, because it's bound to be an interesting ride.

I had debated with myself for many years whether to leave my chosen career in pursuit of something else or to continue with a career that, despite feeling unhappy, I seemed to have a natural affinity for. It was also at a point where I was starting to make really good money.

But here's the thing, when you wake up and go to work every day feeling like you have a noose tightening around your neck, you know eventually you must find a way out, or else you will suffocate and die.

After seven years in an industry that had been raked over the coals in a government banking enquiry and subsequent new rules and regulations enforced upon them, many that went well beyond logic, I was over it.

What started out as a passion for helping people with their finances, had turned into a soul draining compliance regime that had me spending more time ticking boxes than actually helping my clients.

I had known for years now that the only thing keeping me there was my love for my clients and the desire not to let them down. Eventually though, I had to admit it was time to take another leap of faith and trust that I would be guided to what I was to do next.

A Twist Of Fate

Having faith had always come through for me in the past and it was about to prove itself again.

I love how when you openly declare something to the universe, it takes no time in responding if you are in complete alignment with what you're asking for.

My pivotal turning point came unexpectedly at 6am one morning at the gym. I was about to step onto the treadmill when I received a phone call from a friend, seeking out my advice on the guy she had just started dating. As she launched into 'this amazing connection and what the problem was', I spent the next twenty minutes of my gym workout, coaching and guiding her through this experience.

I'd had many conversations like this over the years as a life coach, but this one turned out to be the catalyst for the change I had been waiting for. Whilst the conversation went well and my friend was grateful for my advice, I mistakenly joked to her that this is what I charge my clients for, and she should consider this her 'one free session'. Her adverse reaction that I would even hint at charging a friend was so strong that you'd be mistaken for thinking I had asked for her to hand over her life savings.

However, this conversation led to another conversation with a different friend and before I knew it, I'd fallen out with two friends in the space of two days.

Recognising this as what I like to refer to as a 'tower' moment, I asked myself, "Why is this happening for me?", instead of the usual question most people ask which is, "Why is this happening to me?"

The answer came loud and clear a few short hours later when I realised that despite having been a financial divorce coach, money coach and life coach for approximately four years, I didn't have any formal qualifications other than 'real life' experience. At an unconscious level, I felt unworthy to truly step away from being a fully qualified and experienced financial adviser and take the leap of faith to know that I could make just as good a living – if not better – than what I had now.

It's funny where motivation can come from and for me, it was proving these two friends wrong. Three weeks later, I found myself flying to Brisbane to attend my very first seven-day intensive practitioner training course learning skills in Neurolinguistic Programming (NLP), Time Line Therapy™ and Hypnosis.

From the very first day, I knew without a doubt I was exactly where I was meant to be. At the end of the course, I had not only made the decision to sell my financial planning business in its entirety, I decided the exact date this was going to occur in my future timeline.

Fast forward to Sunday 18th July 2021 and there I was, sitting in front of the person who had agreed to buy my business. We signed the contract, and I couldn't decide if I was excited, nervous, scared or all three.

Three months later, I was doing a whirlwind handover of my business, telling everyone I was taking the next six months off to 'have a break' before launching a new, yet unnamed coaching business.

Well, I got my six months off, just not the way I had planned.

Five weeks into time off, my dad was rushed to hospital with suspected Guillain Barre Syndrome. Within hours, Dad could no longer walk, talk, swallow or breath on his own. As I sat there at his bedside, holding Mum's hand, I was so very grateful that I no longer had a business to run.

My dad did get better, and with a lot of will and determination, he walked out of hospital 10 weeks later, on the road to recovery. Or so we thought.

Four months later, dad was admitted to hospital again, however, this time, it was not long before we all knew he wouldn't be walking out.

Endings And New Beginnings

I used to think everything I had done in business and life up to this point had taken some form of courage. But it was not until I was sitting at my father's bedside in hospital that I learned the true meaning of courage. There he was in the final days of his life and still I hesitated to tell him what I truly wanted to say.

To fully understand, I need to take you back to my childhood. Dad was always just Dad. We never went to him for anything, preferring to ask Mum for fear that Dad would always say no.

The problem was, I was so scared to ask my dad anything that, along the way, I never learned how to communicate with him. Me, the girl who can talk to anyone about anything, was too scared to talk to her own father.

As he lay there in hospital, with it becoming increasingly more evident that he was never going to get better, I began to formulate ways in my mind to tell him everything I had wanted to say my entire life.

Chickening out for the hundredth time, I settled with writing him a five-page letter, pouring out my heart and soul as the tears dripped down onto the page. I carried this letter around in my handbag for two weeks before I finally got the courage to read it to him. Even then, my resolve withered, and, in the end, I sat by his side, holding his hand in complete silence while I read the letter out in my mind only.

Finally, three days before he passed away, I mustered up more courage than I had ever drawn upon before to tell my dad (this time out loud), what I truly wanted him to know before he left this earthly plane.

Sitting there holding his hand, my last conversation with my dad was about how, without ever uttering a word to me about how to build a business, he had taught me from an early age that the most important thing to know is that, "Relationships are key. Have the courage to show up and just be yourself. People will buy from you because they like you, not because you have the best (or cheapest) product."

I never did get to tell my dad anything else I had written in that letter, but it no longer mattered.

What I am glad of, is that I pushed through that fear barrier one more time, plucked up the courage and told him the one thing I knew we both wanted to hear to give us peace before he died and that was how proud I was that he was my dad.

About Me

Hi, my name is Leisa Quagliata, and I am a transformational healing coach and advocate for positive change. I live in North Queensland, Australia with my two gorgeous sons, who as teenagers keep me amused daily.

Over the past seven years, with no financial backing and a strong belief in myself, I built and sold a successful business as a financial adviser, money coach and financial divorce coach. Rocked by multiple personal and professional challenges during this time, I began a personal growth journey that led me in 2021 to sell my business, leave the corporate world behind and begin building a heart-centred, spiritually based business, Connected to Soul.

I now utilise skills as a hypnotherapist, time-line therapist® and NLP practitioner to follow my passion of helping reduce the incidence of male mental health and suicide rate by teaching men how to break free from the life they think they are expected to live.

Having suffered the loss of both my brothers, rising from the ashes of divorce and hitting emotional rock bottoms in 2013 and 2020, I spent most of the past decade soul searching for answers to those all-important questions, "Who am I?" "What am I here for?" and "What is my purpose in life?"

Eventually, I learned that the real secret to living a happy life was healing wounds of the past that keep you feeling trapped in your current life circumstances. When this is achieved, you become limitless in your potential.

Serendipitous events led me to becoming an author after I openly declared to the universe that I was ready to write a book and loudly asked for a sign. Hours later an unexpected turn of events had me digging through the junk mail of my former business, where I found an email from the Queens In Business Club Co-Founder Chloë Bisson titled, "Do you want to write a book with me?"

I dedicate this chapter to my late father Charlie (1945-2022) whose recent passing taught me one of my greatest lessons in courage.

"Have the
lady balls
to stand up"

Shim Ravalia
The Health Queen

I Won't Be Silenced

Jo-Jo Singh
Entrepreneur and Public Speaker
Together We Made It

"Go to the edge of the cliff and jump off. Build your wings on the way down." – Ray Bradbury

Trigger Warning[1]

I am the youngest of four or six depending on how you look at it. I would love to tell you that I have a super supportive and loving family who have encouraged me to be the greatest version I could ever be, however I would be lying.

One thing my parents did pass down to me, however, was to have an appreciation for nature with my mum's love of plants and my dad's fascination with animals.

The biggest lesson I have learned in my life is how to be respectful, grateful and resilient – even the first three days of my life were tough, spent in an incubator with my temperature being extremely low.

As a child, although I had all the materialistic joys in abundance, I lacked emotional guidance. I was also slower in my academic abilities in comparison to my sisters and it made

---

[1] Suicidal ideation

me feel like I was always in a different realm. There is a fine line between banter and straight-up insults and jealousy.

I used to believe that we had the right to judge until I started hearing voices and losing complete control. Things spiraled and I found myself entering a guilty plea in the dock being judged at Southwark Crown Court in 2019.

But I'm getting ahead of myself…

Going Through The Storm
What was 21st June 2018 like for you? Do you remember where you were, who you were with and what clothes you were wearing? This may sound like a random question, and unless this date has some significance to you other than being the longest day of the year, you would not have any memory of it.

For me, it was the date my life changed forever.

I had been going through depression, sleeping so much that my sister thought it was hilarious to get me a 'nap queen' plaque. I could have had another that said 'fridge raider' because that was all I was able to do, being on a cocktail of antidepressants and antipsychotics with the combination of recreational drugs to reduce the side effects of the medication (this is what I believed at the time).

21st June 2018 was the day two female officers came to arrest me for blackmail.

Blackmail. I did not know it was a real thing, I mean how many times have you watched a TV programme and the characters do this with no repercussions? Welcome to the real world.

Surely I cannot be the only person on this planet who has ever felt lost and guilty for doing something that, at the time, felt like the right thing, even though I knew it was the wrong thing.

At the time, I was in what felt like my first ever proper relationship that was so confusing and toxic it makes the inconsistency of the British weather and global warming seem completely normal. I wasn't in a good place, and had been feeling suicidal for the second time, after all, I have always been convinced I have not graduated life to become a resident in prison. Already feeling suicidal, I promised myself not to have a second attempt following my failed attempt at aged eighteen.

Have you ever been wanting so much to change that you find it unbelievably difficult to make the right decision? Fear starts to creep in and your heart feels like it is beating to the drum of everything in the room.

Have you ever put your trust and faith in people that you thought had your best interests at heart, but did not? Looked for advice and guidance from those around you, only to have your dreams dampened due to their disbelief?

I had been silenced for most of my life. And for once I wanted to stand up for myself. But being in a dark place had led me to make some wrong decisions. And that's where entering my guilty plea for blackmail came from.

Luckily, I am proud to state that I have never spent a day in prison. Instead, I was issued a six month suspended sentence with two years' probation.

Powerless

In 2021, I started working 12 hour night shifts for a company called Farmdrop Limited. It has never been part of my plan to work nights, however like many others, the pandemic had pushed me to do things I never thought I would need to do.

Working nights took its toll on my overall health and wellbeing, and my godmother had taken her final breaths just three days before my thirty-sixth birthday. This year was going to be different.

Seven weeks beforehand, I had booked my driving theory test and had been fortunate enough to have been able to book it on my birthday itself. I put all my efforts into practice and focused on passing. Failure was not an option. Well, I am not going to sit here and deny the possibility, but on the day I was booking my test, I came across a website that offered multiple attempts at the test for an additional pound difference.

I called my trusted Auntie O and she stated that there is no need to waste the extra £1 knowing that it was a no brainer and I would pass. So with that in mind the only people that were aware of my test were my aunt, best friend and work colleagues. Many times before I have shared with family members of what I had planned to do or wanted to do and it was the ever so frequent eye roll coupled with a smirk of, "Oh here we go again."

I was so focused on my end goal that even when I found out that my godmother had died, my mind could not process this information because I had held off learning how to drive for such a long time. Nothing and nobody was going to stand in the way of my destination.

I am proud to say I passed, but after that, the reality of what had just happened in my life started to kick in. I remember sitting in the church at the funeral and not one tear fell from my eyes. I was numb, detached and feeling heartless as I watched many others share condolences and memories of the great woman she gracefully was. Instead of attending her wake, I made the decision to attend the House and Garage Orchestra in Chelmsford that evening with the belief that Pat, my godmother, would understand.

A few weeks later, the loss really hit me. In the space of just three years, I had said goodbye to both my grandparents, followed by my dearest unofficial adopted sister Teleba on her birthday, followed by Pat.

For someone who loves to eat, my appetite completely disintegrated. The need for sleep was quickly replaced by overwhelm, confusion, anger, anxiety and daily nightmares. I had no more than two hours of rest for a period of three weeks. Something had to change and I was so desperate for a sudden shift because these patterns had been the triggers for my previous episodes of psychosis in 2014-2016.

Feeling completely powerless and out of control, I was scared to express my thoughts and feelings as I know that those who have seen me in this position before would panic. I did the only thing I could do and that was to reach out to my cousin overseas as this was a person that knew what a mental breakdown was and was also too far to rescue me.

I spoke out and she listened and absorbed every word. I cried and she asked me to remember all the dreams I had for my life. Confused by the question, she told me I need to think and write. Think? All I had been doing was thinking. I wanted to shut my brain off and the only advice she had for me was to think and write. Annoyed by the concept, I abruptly ended the call.

But then I started writing. And I envisioned what I truly wanted.

I had built a strong connection with one of the co-authors from Queens In Business' first book, Time to Reign. Sandra Ammerlaan (Founder of Laugh at Sh*t) kindly invited me to attend Queens In Business' first live event, Reign Like A Queen, after I openly shared my vision with her. There was an opportunity to purchase a VIP ticket which included access to the gala dinner and award ceremony to celebrate the many achievements of the club's members.

I wanted to be in that room, surrounded by multiple people I had not yet met but wanted to learn from so that with time, I too would be privileged enough to be nominated or better yet, receive an award and have my 15 seconds of fame in a loving environment.

Working for a hospitality agency, I had experienced setting up and serving at a variety of VIP gala dinner events for people and I felt the overwhelming need to see what it's like on the other side as an attendee. So it was decided. I was going to throw caution to the wind and attend. I had no idea what I was getting myself into and how this one decision would change the whole trajectory of my life forever.

Powerful

The word 'welcoming' is an understatement when it comes to the Reign Like A Queen event. Maybe 'awe-inspiring' is a closer match. As soon as I was immersed in, I just wanted to scoop up the whole experience and never miss a chance to learn more.

On the last day of the event, I had the chance to invest in Global Success' three-day Professional Speaker School – something I had always wanted to do.

Before this, my belief was that only those who are weak cry in public spaces and those who shared their personal pain and struggles were only looking for attention. After training at speaker school, I now understand that neither of these beliefs are true.

The training was one of the most emotional experiences of my life. I had to stand up in front of complete strangers and share my story. Which part of my story was going to fit the bill?

I sat with another attendee, Julie Fitzpatrick, Founder of Millieside Therapy & Coaching, and I expressed what I thought I was going to share. She took one look into my soul and said that isn't what I am passionate about. I broke down.

I don't know where it came from but I shared my anger at the fact that there are so many young people who feel exiled from reality to the point that they are absorbed into gaming and drugs as a means of escapism. These are experiences that I have had in my past. Julie had helped me unlock what truly lights a fire within me and what I can speak up about to help others.

On the final day, we had to stand in front of a group and give a 25 minute talk. Fear engulfed me and I ran out of the room bawling my eyes out in the most uncontrollable form.

A couple of the mentors found me and empowered me to continue. I was asked to identify where exactly in my body I needed my inner power to come from. In that moment, my stomach felt as though it was sparking a fire of the power I was in need of. Deep breaths fueled with maximum power to help me deliver my talk.

For the first time, I spoke about the darkest moments of my existence. No longer scared of judgement, the words were flowing so smoothly that I can only describe it as an out-of-body experience. The audience was silent. I had their full undivided attention. As I looked into their eyes, I could see the same tears that I had just moments before.

My time was up and the feedback was unforgettable.

"You have a gift."

"This is your story of empowerment that can save lives."

There was no judgement, just respect. Embarrassment no longer lived in my world and I returned home feeling like a huge weight had finally lifted. I had forgiven myself for the part I played in the events that unfolded and tarnished my name in my past. Now a different form of fear was waiting for me.

Winners Never Quit And Quitters Never Win
Like a light switch, severe depression was everywhere. Sleeping too much, eating not enough and hiding from the world. Crisis team on speed dial. I lost control again.

Unequipped, running out of solutions. A referral back to the mental health team and just like that an appointment was booked to speak with a psychiatrist.

Adamant to never go back on medication that had always turned rain into a full blown natural disaster for me, I had been off my medication for over a year. There was no way I was going to return to that numbing state that made everyone around me super happy and comfortable, except for me.

Ignored, a prescription was written. It was like she was working on commission to get these tablets back into my system. But the universe was on my side and she forgot to state what type she was prescribing me. That meant I was advised to return to the psychiatrist which was a chance for me to stand strong again. The ball was now in my court and I worked on regaining a healthy balance.

Around this time, Happiness Doctor Francis Ikhenemoh (who was within one of my business networks) had just published his first book, Depression Lies. If anyone really knew what I was going through and could relate to my current situation, it was him. It was like the universe knew. I asked him for some advice and the answer was so simple that it made me wonder how I had missed it all along.

Exercise, fresh air, food that puts a smile on my face and good sleep is the best combination and alternative to medication.

Another tonne of weight lifted from me.

Many times in my life, I have ignored my heart out of fear of being judged and that has been my biggest downfall. I wasn't going to let this happen again.

A New Outlook

Courage to me is stepping into the unknown and seeing how things go with complete trust and faith in making a decision. Instead of asking, "What if things go wrong?", I now wonder, "What if things go right?"

I have spent the majority of my life looking for validation from others and getting their approval on whether or not what I choose to do will be accepted by them. And for many of those people, be it close friends or family members, the things that I would stand up and say scared them so much that they would tell me my dreams are silly and impossible. That I am not equipped to do something like that.

To be different, you have to move different. Change your circle of influence and you are sure to start seeing mega improvements.

You are the sum of the five people you hang around. I give credit to Stacey Flowers for breaking this down during her Ted Ex talk. She described the five people you need to have in your circle for growth:

1. Mentor
2. Coach
3. Cheerleader

4. Friend

5. Peer

Queens In Business Club Co-Founder Chloë Bisson once told me that in order to have a successful business, you need to have a healthy mind because a business is only as successful as the people in it.

Go to where people give you the space to be you. I mean the real you. We only have one life to live and the mistakes we make form our character.

The difference between school and life is that in school, you learn the lesson and then take the test. Life works the opposite way round. Don't do what I did and exist without living, silencing your voice to allow others to feel comfortable while you suffer inside.

What is meant to be for you will always be there for you to achieve no matter how many dead ends and wrong turns you take. Keep going, pause, breathe, reset and go.

If there is one thing I have learnt in my life, it is that the mind is the most powerful force in the world. Right now in this moment, I want you to do me a huge favour and look around the room you are in. Everything you see came from someone's mind. Every item started off as an idea.

I am sure you have heard the expression, 'there is no I in team'. The word team for me means Together Each Action Matters.

There is not one person who achieved greatness and success on their own. A seed needs a combination of earth, water and sunlight to flourish.

However, take into consideration that if you place a plant in the wrong sized pot it is possible to stifle its growth. Why am I telling you this? The point I am making here is that you are never on your own and neither should you isolate yourself in whatever you are going through. Reaching out and asking for help shows *courage*.

About Me

Born and raised in North London, I predominately grew up on the border of Hackney and Tottenham. I spent a major part of my early childhood alone, writing stories which all featured the word 'lost' in the title.

I wrote this chapter because I needed to share with you that it does not matter how many times you make mistakes or how slow you progress. Remember, the tortoise has the ability to live for over 100 years, simply by taking baby steps.

Perfection does not exist either. The more time spent attempting to attain it, the more you will realise that it is holding you back, but that is okay. The best way to learn is by making mistakes because that is where you grow. Invest in you. Your personal development is everything in this world. Find a mentor and enrol into a mind gym daily. Do not underestimate your capability. Find a community of like-minded individuals who empower you and when needed, borrow their belief in you.

During a counselling session I was told that I am a rose surrounded by weeds and not to forget I have thorns. For some time I thought this was true, until I realised I am not a rose in a pretty garden. In fact, I am an acorn who had fallen from a giant oak tree and hit some mighty rocks on the way down. And now finally, I have planted myself in a strong foundation, been showered in the rain and am ready to grow tall in the midst of the beautiful forest of greatness.

I dedicate this to the reader, to my fur baby Wiley-Kit as he has been my loyal companion in my darkest hours, and to Julie for all the amazing RTT coaching work on my mindset and growth.

Carrie Griffiths' Five Tips For Building A Courageous Voice

Carrie Griffiths
Voice and Transformational Coach
Carrie Griffiths Voice Training

"I believe that if you'll just stand up and go, life will open up for you." – Tina Turner

"Loud women are not feminine."

"Speak up, I can't hear you!"

"Stop screeching!"

How many times have you been told, or heard other women receive these types of comments?

Multiple studies have shown that adult males naturally prefer lower-pitched voices, whereas babies and children naturally prefer higher-pitched voices.

Lower-pitched voices represent strength and security, whereas to an adult human, a high-pitched voice represents femininity and youth. With all this confusion around what's attractive to whom, heteronormative interpretations, and biased societal opinions around how women should represent themselves, it's no wonder that some of us don't feel able to speak up for ourselves or speak out when we need to.

Well I bring good news. From personal experience, I can say that speaking with courage doesn't mean conforming to the opinions of a bunch of people you will probably never meet. It's something that you can learn fairly quickly and practice daily - and it doesn't have to be a chore.

As a shy extrovert I've always loved being in and around large groups of people and especially loved being on stage. But I found it extremely difficult to strike up or even continue conversations with people. And being in a number of toxic personal and professional relationships where I wasn't allowed to speak my mind, it became more and more difficult the older I got.

Knowing that I would have to learn to network if I were to build a successful singing career, I learned how to interact appropriately with other people, how to engage them in interesting conversations, and leave knowing that they would remember me in a positive light.

Tip #1: Understand That Your Voice Is Beautiful!
You are the only person who will ever have your voice. It can't be recreated by robots or given to someone else. Okay larynx (voice box) transplants are possible (that's a chapter in itself!) but once implanted in someone else, that voice would not sound like you. Even if you have a twin or more multiple birth siblings, you all have nuances that make your voices unique to you. And no matter how similar you sound, you can bet that at least one of your close family can tell you apart just by how your voice sounds.

If you've grown up believing your voice sounds unpleasant, or you've been told your voice is annoying, or even if your voice has changed after pregnancy or menopause, and you're wondering what happened to that other person with the 'prettier' voice, take comfort knowing that however you feel about it right now, you can improve your relationship with your voice without too much effort.

Fall in love with your imperfections. A stammer held me back for many years. When I started mentioning my stammer, most people I had known for years said that they'd never noticed it. To be fair they'd probably just gotten used to it because my college students can definitely spot it when they meet me for the first time! My point is, you don't have to speak perfectly for people to be interested in what you have to say.

After all, perfect is boring.

Tip #2: Take Your Time
You'd be surprised how much your tongue, teeth and lips (the articulators) get in the way when you speak. Let's face it, the shape of your mouth plays a big part in your accent, so it makes sense that your articulators are important for clear and confident speaking.

People who speak the Queen's English (Queen Elizabeth II, the current reigning monarch, not the QIB Co-Founders!) are said to 'speak with a plum in their mouth'. That is because the way you shape your mouth to speak 'proper' English is similar to the shape your mouth would make if you were holding a whole plum in it. Now I don't know about you but that doesn't paint an elegant picture, even if one considers the sound majestic.

When you take note of the many ways your tongue, teeth and lips form words - your diction - it's easy to see how they can get in the way when you feel flustered or can't remember what it is that you want to say.

The way you speak is unique to you and I, personally, don't believe in 'fixing' quirks like a lisp or a stammer. I have learned to embrace my stammer, and though it has lessened more recently, it is part of me and my story.

Diction, tone and colour are different and equally important elements of your speaking patterns. Speaking slightly more slowly will give people a chance to hear and process everything you say, allowing you to build rapport and keep them interested. It also means you won't have to keep repeating yourself and tire your voice out!

Fun activity: watch yourself speaking in front of a mirror – maybe read this section out loud - and try and count how many different movements your tongue, teeth and lips make!

Tip #3: Speak With Your Mouth, Not Your Throat!

This is possibly the most important tip I can give you in terms of being confident about making yourself heard while looking after your voice.

You see, where most people fall down vocally, whether they're speaking or singing, is that they try to create sound in their throat. It makes sense that you would, seeing as that is where your larynx is located.

"What the heaven is she talking about?" I hear you cry.

Confident speaking requires a confident sounding voice, and this is where you could come unstuck.

Most people who are conscious about their voice for one reason or another – whether it's because they use it for work, because they don't like the sound of it and are trying to change it, or because they are trying to project or speak louder – try to use their throat to speak. With your larynx (voice box) located in your throat you'd be forgiven for believing that you should use your throat to talk.

However, people who have taken voice training are distinguishable by the tone, colour, smoothness, and fullness of their voice. They know that using your throat to talk only puts strain on your vocal folds (vocal cords) and the muscles in and around your larynx, creating tension (the enemy of a strong, healthy voice) and eventually causing damage. And to top it off, your voice ends up sounding worse.

But, while your vocal cords are indeed inside your larynx, the sound should travel from your throat and resonate in different places. You can learn to manipulate where the sound is made quite easily.

Silly game: Try mimicking Mr Bean's voice, or Mickey Mouse's. Both implement simple techniques I use as a voice coach to help people to improve their speaking voices. Plus, they're fun to mimic!

Tip #4: Your Voice Is NOT Made Of Steel!
I'd be a terrible voice coach if I didn't include a tip about looking after your voice. What I'm about to say may sound harsh. I say it with love and the very best intentions.

Overworking your voice because you're speaking too long, or too loudly, or just not using it in the right way can cause irreparable damage, or at the very least damage that takes longer to fix than it did to cause.

I'm constantly shocked and frustrated by speakers and coaches who proudly announce that they're going to have 'no voice' by the end of their presentation or program. That isn't something to be proud of, it's something that needs to be addressed. If you have no voice left at the end of a two or three hour presentation, you're doing something wrong. Used correctly, the quality of your voice should improve with time, rather than diminish.

Most of the coaches and speakers I'm around on a day-to-day basis have very poor vocal health and some are a presentation away from f*cking up their voices permanently. Sorry, not sorry.

I'm similar to a doctor in that most coaches and speakers seek help from me when the damage is already done, meaning it takes longer to fix than it does to train. In cases where serious damage has occurred I have to refer my clients to a voice therapist for weeks, or even months of rehabilitation before I can help them to use their voices properly. It's like a boxer going into the ring with no training; they're going to get battered. You wouldn't do it to your body, so why are you doing it to your voice?

I could trail off a list of high-profile speakers and coaches whom, had they worked with a voice coach in the early days, they most likely would not have developed the irreversible voice issues they have today.

I'm known for my catchphrase 'stay hydrated', but hydration alone won't save your voice. Other things to consider when speaking at length is your volume. If you need to speak louder, invest in a good quality lapel, hand-mic or headset that you carry around with you, the same way singers do. While a microphone isn't a replacement for good vocal technique, it will save you from having to raise your voice above background noise or low-quality equipment.

I don't mean to scare you off, especially as this is supposed to inspire courage – I'm saying this to help you. PLEASE look after your voices.

And for heaven's sake, stop trying to speak from your diaphragm.

Let Loose: Go through a quick body scan from the crown of your head, noticing all of the places you feel tense, and relax each part of your body, including the palms of your hands and the soles of your feet, before an important conversation or presentation, or entering a room full of people.

Bonus tip: If you really can't get through the day without coffee, I recommend alternating with warm honey, lemon and ginger on long speaking days. Oh, and never drink cold water with ice!

If you use your voice for work, as most of us do, either as a professional speaker, in constant meetings, consulting with or coaching clients, or you are a specialist voice worker, I highly recommend working with a qualified and experienced voice coach who can help you get the best from your voice without abusing it.

A regular vocal warm up routine can take as little as two minutes and save years of stress, frustration, pain and rehabilitation.

Tip #5: Believe In What You're Saying

When you speak from a place of truth and love, you can never go wrong. People may not always agree with what you're saying but you won't ever feel guilty about what you say, because it's true for you. The caveat here is to be respectful of their human rights and dignity, and to not take the way others respond personally.

It can take courage to speak your truth, so always remember to only say what you're comfortable saying. If you're sharing something traumatic, be kind to yourself and share only the things that you have dealt with and won't be triggered by. It can help to have some supporting data, even if it's just an opinion held by many people. Try using phrases like:

"In my experience…"
"I've learned that…"
"It's my belief that…"

This makes it clear that it's something that you believe to be true and not an idea you're trying to force others to agree with.

Most importantly…

Remember that what you have to say is important. Because when you respect what you have to say and the voice you're saying it with, others will too.

Stay hydrated.

About Me

I am the Founder of Carrie Griffiths Voice Training, and a London-based singer, international speaker and multi-award winning voice coach, specialising in commercial singing, and conversational and public speaking.

Having been a successful singer for more than twenty years, I have performed in over thirty countries to audiences of thousands, and sold three top ten albums, including a number one.

I have used these experiences to create a dynamic voice training system that helps singers, coaches and speakers to develop healthier, beautiful sounding voices that enhance their on-stage presence, make a bigger impact and maximise profits.

I'd like to thank my mum, and the rest of my family, who always support and encourage me - even if they don't fully understand what the heaven it is that I'm doing!

Surviving To Thriving

Teresa Steuart-Pownall
Owner and Manager
The Haven

"Never bend your head. Hold it high. Look the world straight in the eye." – Helen Keller

Trigger Warning[1]

I am a fifty-five year old holistic, beauty and aesthetic practitioner, and the Owner and Manager of The Haven hair and beauty salon in St. Leonards-on-Sea, East Sussex.

I truly believe that the trauma in my past shaped my future and these experiences made me the person I am today. It makes me want to help everyone that I come into contact with who has had similar experiences. If it was not for my past then I would not be the Owner of my salon and would have followed my teenage dreams of being an artist or something similar instead.

But that's not how it worked out for me.

I grew up in St. Leonards-On-Sea with four brothers and one sister. Much later, my parents went on to have another set of twins but the age gap was 20 years between myself and my twin brothers. We lived in a council house in a nice area and

---

[1] Sexual abuse

although we were always fed, money was tight and there were no luxuries.

My dad ran a very strict household and I was extremely frightened of the consequences if I misbehaved. There was physical, mental and – from the age of 10 – sexual abuse.

I grew up being told by my dad that my purpose in life as a woman was to marry, have children and look after my husband. I was told throughout life that I was stupid. I remember when I was about thirteen at a parent's evening, the teacher praised my artwork and said I should go to art college when I leave school. Outside the school however, my dad told me not to have any fancy ideas about that as I was not good enough.

Consequently, I did not take any exams in my final year as I saw no point, and the day after leaving school, I started work in a local factory. Earning money gave me a bit more freedom but I was not happy working there. I tried another factory and lasted a week, then went to work in a care home which I enjoyed. I started working as many hours as I could to keep out of the way of my dad but he told me to reduce the hours, and I knew what it would mean if I didn't!

My dad was a violent, controlling bully who only allowed me out one evening a week. If I had any dates, my boyfriend had to pick me up from home and have me back by 9pm. He made sure none of these dates ever lasted very long.

With a job bringing in some money, I felt like I had an opportunity to escape the constant abuse, so one day after payday, I got on a train to London. I was lucky that I found somewhere to stay and got a new job the very same day.

Unfortunately for me though, I got into a relationship with a guy who was an alcoholic and handy with his fists. A friend advised me to leave and go back to my parents. She said she was concerned and would contact them if I did not go back. I felt I had no choice, so returned home after 10 months away.

At this point, I was three months pregnant at seventeen!

I dreaded having to go home but I had nowhere else to go, and staying in London was not an option. When I returned, my parents were pleased to see me and my mum was very supportive during my pregnancy. They were overjoyed at becoming grandparents when my son Daniel was born in October 1984.

Fast forward a couple of years and I had saved enough to move out and also met my first husband. We secretly dated and when we found a flat, I went home to my parents and announced that I was moving out the following day.

My husband was much older than me and adored the ground I walked on but by the time I was thirty, I felt suffocated as he wanted me to stay home and look after the house. I wanted to look for work and although I did, my husband was unhappy. We separated and divorced.

I had no friends and decided to kill two birds with one stone by going to my local college open day with a view to meet new people and prove to myself that I was not stupid! I really believed after a lifetime of being told that I was stupid that maybe I was.

I looked through the prospectus and saw the beauty course which interested me. When I enrolled, I asked the tutor if there was additional learning help as I felt that I would need it. The tutor suggested going to a class they were running to assess what help I would need. I went along and after doing an assessment, the tutor asked me why I thought I needed assistance. I told her I thought I would struggle with the course as I was not very bright. She looked at me with a shocked expression and told me I would sail through the course but if I did need any help, I should contact her.

One year later, I passed with flying colours!

Following this, I did eight diplomas over seven years at Hastings College and also received a student of the year award. Thinking I was stupid led me to train in beauty and massage and consequently led me to start my business!

To date I have 37 qualifications in my field and recently I completed a vaccinator course with St John Ambulance so that I can volunteer for the NHS and give the Covid-19 vaccine.

Facing my demons, or should I say demon, gave me the courage to stand up for myself and carve a better life.

This fight is what gave me the courage to stand up in court and give evidence against my dad for the years of abuse I suffered as a child. It was a horrendous time, from reporting it to the police, to the case actually getting to court, as my dad pulled every trick in the book to stop the trial going ahead. At times, I wondered if it ever would.

My mum was with me every step of the way and I could not have done it without her. When he was sentenced to 21 years in prison, I could finally put my past behind me and move on with my life.

Creating The Haven

Within my business, my role involves everything from performing treatments and reception duties to marketing, cleaning and everything in between to keep the business running. I absolutely love my job and I am very passionate about giving my clients the best treatments they have ever had, making them return time after time.

I also offer accredited courses at the salon to pass on my knowledge, having completed a teaching diploma in June 2020. I feel it is important to train in new treatments on a regular basis so that you keep up with the latest trends and to also not become complacent.

I decided to train in aesthetic treatments in 2021 and I was lucky to find a local trainer, Tracy from The Little White Rooms, to complete three courses with. I was very nervous on the first course as it was Vitamin B12 injections and even when I got to the training venue, I was asking myself what on earth I was doing here! I gave myself a talking to and promised myself that if I did not enjoy the course, then I would not offer the service at the salon. Well, I needn't have worried because I absolutely loved it!

My motto within the business is: don't ask anyone to do something that you would not do yourself (hence why I clean the salon thoroughly after work).

My vision for The Haven is somewhere clients can come to unwind, offload and be pampered, giving them a 'home away from home' feel.

But before starting my current business, I was happy working as an aromatherapy therapist visiting residential homes for adults with learning difficulties. At the same time, I was running a small mobile beauty business on the side. After being inundated with male customers wanting more than just a massage, that dream was whittled down. It was just not safe!

Then, a friend from college asked me if I would be interested in opening a salon with her. I liked the idea and said I would think about it. The seed was planted and the more I thought about it, the more excited I got about the prospect of opening a salon.

I decided that if I opened it with my friend, then at least we would have each other to bounce ideas off and the risk would be halved. I was single at the time so would still need to have a reliable income until the business started making a profit. So I would work part-time as an aromatherapy therapist and spend my 'two days off' cramming in several cleaning jobs.

We started looking for suitable premises. After months of nothing becoming available, my friend rang me excitedly one weekend and said she had seen an advert in a local paper for a salon for rent. We viewed it the same day, and although the landlord found out we had never run a business before, he allowed us to rent the premises!

We were given a month's free rent so that we could decorate and revamp, ready to open in July 2008.

My biggest challenge in my business journey so far was in November 2009 when my business partner asked if we could have a chat…We met the following day and she announced that she was leaving. She had taken legal advice and did not want to continue with the business. I asked the dreaded question of when she planned to leave and she replied, "Tomorrow!"

Obviously, I was shocked but also realised her heart was not in it. I told her I understood but that I would need some time to get legal advice. We had no contract – big mistake!

I had invested too much time and money in the business to just give up so I decided to try going solo. It was tough but I managed with the help of friends and family, especially my lovely mum who had separated from my dad many years before and became my receptionist. She also looked after the salon one afternoon a week whilst I went off to a cleaning job. Keeping the business going was the best thing I have done and I have never looked back.

Are You Okay?
While at work on 21st January 2018 – a day before my birthday – I was in the middle of doing a treatment and felt unwell. I tried soldiering on but really started to feel that I needed to sit down. I asked the client if she would mind, and she replied, "No but are you okay?"

I wasn't, but I told her it was probably just a bit of indigestion or a bug that was doing the rounds.

Anyway, apparently I looked quite grey so the clients and hairdresser decided to call an ambulance. My thoughts at the time were, oh my god, I am going to look a right idiot when they turn up. I was then whisked away, still wondering what all the fuss was about.

Several hours later I was told that I had had a heart attack and needed to stay in hospital to find out what was wrong. I had two stents fitted and was in hospital for a week.

I knew by the end of the week that things would have to change with the business, I had been burning the candle at both ends, stressing about an issue with the landlord and basically smoking far too much.

I eased myself back into work gradually, again friends came to the rescue and covered the shifts at the salon. My hairdresser at the time was amazing and looked after the running of it. I cut my hours down drastically, stopped stressing about things and started having some hobbies as I realised up until then that all I did was run the business. I had no hobbies.

My health scare had prompted me to reevaluate. But this experience was nothing compared to what happened in November 2018.

Although it did not feel like it at the time, this is when I felt I had the most courage. Yet it was also the most devastating time of my life.

A couple of weeks before I was due to get married, I realised that something was wrong with my mum, but I hoped I was wrong. I will be forever grateful that she was able to attend my wedding as she was so happy that I had my husband, Nick, by my side. I know she worried about me not having that special someone.

In December of 2018, I took my mum to the appointment at the hospital to find out the results of her tests. We were then told the devastating news that she had stage four lung cancer and just months to live.

I had to drop her home and return to work. I'm not sure how I managed to work that afternoon but my mum told me I must go, despite me feeling my world had collapsed.

The next few months were horrendous. Part of me wishes I had closed the business while my mum deteriorated but she had made me promise that I would not let it affect the business. When she came to stay with me in February 2019, my business became my escape from reality and then it really was my haven.

My mum was so proud of my achievements and told everyone that she came into contact with that I had my own business. I had to get through this for her as I did not want to let her down.

Between night shifts and looking after my mum, I do wonder how on earth I managed the last couple of months going to work with only a few hours of sleep. I am not sure if it was courage, but going to work with a smile on your face while knowing your world is crashing down around you is very difficult, to say the least.

My mum passed away on 2nd April 2019.

Making Her Proud
The following year was my proudest in business.

I entered the Great British Entrepreneur Awards for Health and Wellbeing in the South East. Looking at previous winners, I honestly thought we had no hope of being picked. When I received an email saying that we were one of the four finalists, I was blown away!

Sadly, we did not win but the whole experience was so uplifting, we got press coverage and an excuse to dress up for the awards ceremony even if it was on Zoom. It was the first award I had entered and I loved the experience so much that I will be entering more.

Throughout my journey, I have faced many struggles and heartache. But I am proud of my resilience and drive to move forward.

I always used to hear the word damaged when people spoke about abuse victims and it really upset me, almost like their lives are ruined and their future's bleak. Well, I am certainly not damaged nor my life bleak. I am proof that anything is possible if you want it.

To the next generation of female entrepreneurs, I say follow your dreams! If you want to start a business it can become reality. It is not easy but if you do your research and arm yourself with the abilities needed for that business, then you can do it.

Write a business plan. Network and meet fellow business owners, get tips from them, join supportive communities like the Queens In Business Club, have a strategy and do not rush into it.

Be passionate about the business you want to start – after all you're going to spend a fair amount of time doing it. If possible, start while you are still employed or have a backup fund in case times are hard or you have unexpected expenses.

In reading my story, I hope I have inspired you to recognise that no matter what life throws at you or whether people say you're not good enough, bright enough or that you won't make it – if you really want it, go for it.

I took the steps after 30 years of being told I was stupid and not good enough and if I can do it so can you!

Life has been tough with ups and downs but my business is flourishing and I hope this gives you the push to start your business.

About Me

I am Teresa Steuart-Pownall, also known as Topcat or TC.

I am the owner and manager of The Haven hair and beauty salon based in St. Leonards-On-Sea for the last 14 years. I absolutely love my job and am passionate about delivering the very best treatments to my wonderful clients.

Before the salon, I was an aromatherapist travelling to residential homes to give massages to adults with learning difficulties whilst training at Hastings College, where I had various private cleaning jobs and also did care work.

I was born in Weymouth and moved to St. Leonards-On-Sea when I was about two years old. I am married to Nick and I have one son, Daniel, and a sixteen year old grandson, Liam.

I have six brothers, one sister and 15 nieces and nephews. Not forgetting my favourite Uncle Rob, also known as Ginger. I have two fur babies, both boxers: Ruby who is seven and Bosley who is five.

I love travelling, especially city breaks, and Italy is my favourite country so far. I intend to see as much of the world as possible. I am a real foodie so eating out is another passion and I love trying out new foods when I am abroad.

I took the leap to be in the Queens In Business book to share my story and hopefully inspire other women to follow their dreams. A special mention to Casey and Elise whom I am very proud of.

I dedicate this chapter to my beautiful mum, Mary Davis, who was my rock, my confidant, my best friend and I will always be your Sunday girl! I will miss you forever.

"Feel fear and allow it to *fuel you* not control you"

Chloë Bisson
The Automation Queen

Face Life With Fortitude

Ruth Oliver
Owner
East UK Accountants (City) Ltd

"With determination we shall succeed." – Franklin D. Roosevelt

The words written on a fridge magnet that I look at each day remain clear, although the picture accompanying the words is faded with age:

Ruth
From the Hebrew meaning "friend of beauty".
She is strong, dedicated, well respected and hardworking;
She will fight for those she loves.
A born leader.

Two close friends in different decades of my life gave me the gift of these words, defining the characteristics of a woman named Ruth which are interwoven with my past and the new experiences in my life to this day.

The words themselves originate from the lessons of the Old Testament Book of Ruth in the Bible.

As you read these words, let's take a brief journey together enabling you to glimpse the impact that many amazing people have, and continue to have on my life, interwoven with the woman I have become through the choices I have made in life. The standards, beliefs, and values that have shaped the person I am today.

An Idyllic Start

I was a much longed-for first child, born eight years after my parents had married. Mother was gentle and caring, and having me had not been easy – yet it was Dad who decided he could not face another pregnancy. Dad was the centre of my world and gave me all the love and devotion any child could need and more.

It was rare for me to be in the company of children of my own age prior to going to primary school. The first years of my life were spent mainly in the company of adults, and even when I was with the children of my parent's friends and cousins in the family, I was always the youngest. It was no surprise for me to have learnt to walk, talk and acquire a varied vocabulary long before I was one year old. Before going to school at the age of five I was reading books and able to do sums that required a knowledge of basic arithmetic.

My father was the estate manager of the Hampden House Estate in Brentwood. The estate, which covered vast acres of land running between both Woodman Road and Seven Arches Road, was owned by a single lady. We lived in a cottage with extensive grounds that were within the estate, and also adjacent to Woodman Road.

In celebration of my birth the lady transferred the title deeds for the cottage and its grounds to my parents. I recall being carried on my dad's shoulders through Hampden Woods on many a day to spend a happy hour laughing, giggling and chatting with the lady in the beautiful drawing room of her house as he worked.

By the age of four I was privileged to be considered responsible enough to sit on the piano stool and gently touch the keys of the grand piano listening in wonder to the musical tones. The gardens of the house were filled with interesting buildings to explore including the orangerie and greenhouses with established grape vines. An expansive lawn approached the summerhouse where we often sheltered when it rained.

The summerhouse was rendered white and had steps leading up to it, with Greek columns and rooms housing what, for me, were new treasures to play with on either side. Rajah, the first golden retriever in my life, belonged to the lady but happily accompanied my father and myself as we walked through the grounds of established plants and trees. I tried to be useful and help, often carrying buckets, small trowels and forks, digging the soil and moving plants alongside my father.

In addition to the house, there was the garden of the cottage to explore along with many animals which included Tiger the cat, ducks, and chickens. The geese followed me around as if they were my guard dog alerting my parents if anything unusual was happening with the noise they made.

The first year of school was an idyllic mix of new experiences. The teacher was young and had only just completed her training. She was gentle and did not correct me when I used my left hand to write across the page. The writing was never very tidy, as until you learn how to cope with positioning your left hand on the page, with small hands it is difficult to leave space to apply the pen as your own hand always seems to be in the way.

My sixth year brought many changes with it. Dad was no longer employed at the house or as the Estate Manager. He was now working shift work at the local Kodak factory opposite our cottage.

The lady now needed a full-time nurse.

For the first time in this year, I experienced the loss of someone that had been close to me and was influential and special in my life. The young teacher who had been so kind did not appear at school at the beginning of the following academic year. It was subsequently announced that she was very ill.

Shortly after this, we were told that she would not be returning, when mum collected me from school, I handed her the sealed letter that had been issued by the Headmistress for us to give to our parents. Mum and Dad sat me down and gently broke the news that she had passed away and was in heaven. I understood that heaven is where God is, a beautiful place of peace and joy, where there is no pain and suffering.

Our class was merged with children that were older. The teacher who was nearing retirement age was very strict and we were required to hand in the result of 100 word spelling tests and recite our times tables each day. She also disapproved of my writing with my left hand and tried to correct it by making me hold the pen in my right hand. I continued to love my reading and sums but writing with my right hand was never going to happen.

My school reports were good, but I became quieter and even more introverted ensuring that I did not receive the punishments meted out to some of the naughty children. It was a different world and approach to that which we see in schools today. With the exception of the fear of corporal punishment, she was an excellent teacher. The education I received and the structure of the days were good for me and a part of my future.

When I attended school, Mum would take me home for lunch each day. If I was to begin to feel ill it was always just before I was due to leave for school giving me an extra day at home. Strangely, I felt better later on in the mornings of those days and happily did my school work and more at home, as well as enjoying time in the garden with the new addition to the family – a small toy poodle, Cindy.

The lady died during my eighth year. The house and estate were left in her will to the China Inland Mission with the intention of the house being used as a children's orphanage. After a period of time, the house and estate were placed in an auction, the highest bidder and new owner was a residential property development company. My parents sold our cottage to the developer who bought the estate at the auction.

I deliberately did not drive through Woodman Road until 2015 when I was travelling into London on a regular basis to visit my clients. The only reminder of the Hampden Estate is the part of Hampden Wood which exists to this day, and the name of the new road, Hampden Crescent. The cottage used to be where the Hampden Crescent turning is on Woodman Road.

Finding My Feet
In 1967, we moved from Brentwood to Colchester. Being torn from everything I had known in the first eight years of my life was impactful in many ways.

We rarely returned to London or Brentwood to visit family or my adopted uncles and aunties, in particular my auntie Gwen and uncle Cyril who had three daughters – Mary, Liddy and their youngest, Ruth – all of whom were several years older than me.

Several times, in completely different places and circumstances in my life, I have found myself reconnected to people that have been important to me many years earlier. I happened to be visiting my friend Ann in a nursing home at Frinton On Sea in 1995 and immediately recognised auntie Gwen, who was staying there with two other friends I knew, Esther and Ena who were wonderful ladies that ran a children's orphanage in Brentwood. I learnt something so important from renewing these connections.

It had been almost 30 years since we had been in close contact but they still loved me. Gwen referred to the bond formed between myself and her three daughters as being part of an extended family. Talking about Dad, she told me that he was so protective of me that it was rare for them or my own mother to be allowed to hold me as he always did.

Ena and Esther held an impromptu birthday party for me that year and told me the stories of the orphans I had known through them who were still their family of adopted children and grandchildren.

When I was thirteen years old, my mother suffered a cerebral haemorrhage and it felt as though I had assumed the full responsibilities of an adult overnight in addition to completing my school work. By this time, I was also working part-time on Saturdays in a shoe shop.

At sixteen, whilst still at school, I already had three paid jobs. The first was the shoe shop, where I worked most Saturdays and also during the school holidays to fill in for full-time members of staff. The second was with the secretary of a local private school, helping her with typing and day-to-day administration tasks. The third was at a local music shop that engaged me as a private tutor for adults who wanted to learn to play the piano.

My income was sufficient to provide for my day-to-day personal expenditure, including shoes, clothes, books, videos and LPs as well as furniture and electrical equipment. By this time, my dad also had his own business and I helped him with his accounting records for the completion of his tax returns as well.

After completing my GCSE exams with good grades, the private school I had been working for offered me a position as Assistant School Secretary, and I was employed full-time there for the next two years.

At the age of eighteen, I had experienced and learnt a lot academically, personally and from the lessons of life the people I was closely connected with had taught me. My 1976 CV already included details of more than five years of experience as an employee, and as a self-employed business owner having worked for the music shop in addition to helping my father with the administration of his business.

When Life Hits You

My first role as a clerical officer at Post Office Telecommunications was in the accounts team who dealt with general customer billing enquiries. After initial training at the local office, every employee was required to complete a three week training course at the in-house training centre located in Birmingham. I already had my own car and drove from Colchester to Birmingham each Sunday, and home again on a Friday evening. Those 15 days spent away from home were my first experience of being on my own.

The training course taught us how to use what were some of the most advanced computer terminals powered by the mainframe systems used within Post Office Telecommunications at that very early stage. Our work was carried out by accessing the billing system through terminals and keyboards on each desk in a normal office environment. This was my first experience with computers and the catalyst leading to my early interest in the power of technology and structured systems.

Each of us was responsible for dealing with around 10,000 customers. We received telephone calls from them, logging the queries to the computer system and progressing these to successful completion. I quickly became proficient and highly effective at answering my customer queries. As a customer advisor I also acquired excellent communication skills that were of tremendous value as part of my work, personal life and professional development.

By 1984 I was substituting for the team manager when she was on leave, and it was August 1984 when I successfully completed a two-year BTEC HNC Course in business and finance.

My corporate career continued to progress and by 1990, I had completed the foundation, and intermediate examinations required to qualify as an ACCA accountant. I took the redundancy package and left British Telecom in April 1991, passing my final ACCA examinations in June.

During this time, with the help of my father, I became the owner of my first property at twenty-two years old. I would not be moving alone as my very own cat Minnie accompanied me.

Two of my friends, Ann and Eva, who regularly visited my home every other Friday evening, had been missionaries to Ghana for more than 30 years. They were both inspirational speakers, and there was a published biography written by Eva about their lives in Africa.

She had a wonderful singing voice. On those evenings I played the piano and sang the songs she had selected for the next meetings. She specifically asked for me to be the pianist accompanying her on multiple occasions. There was a special bond between all three of us. These times were all too short, Eva had a long term health condition and passed away soon after this in 1982.

My father wanted me to move closer to them, and the house in Golden Noble Hill was sold when my parents moved from the family home. It only took five minutes to walk between the two properties we purchased in Prettygate.

In November 1983, my telephone rang at just after 7am in the morning. It was my dad, and the four words he said were, "Your mum is gone". It was a few minutes before he managed to tell me about the ambulance that had taken them both to Essex County Hospital the night before, after she had a second cerebral haemorrhage.

By Christmas, I knew Dad was also extremely unwell. I used to go straight home from work and cook meals for him each day. In a conversation during March of 1984 my father looked at me and said, "How have I made you so independent? And like me you are cautious before you let another person get too close to you."

The first time I understood why what had happened in his own life had such an impact on me was when a friend of mine in 2014 told me about the X chromosome a girl inherits from her father. The X chromosome passes on inherited traits, behaviours, and learnings from the father and his mother as well. That streak of independence and ability to handle any situation I needed to was identical to his own. The passion and absolute sense of purpose and determination I lived my life with mirrored his own. What he omitted to say was, although I would never let another person control me, we both cared deeply for people around us and were there to help those close to us when it mattered most. I learnt the meaning of unconditional love from him as this is what he gave to me from birth until he was reunited with Mum in April, 1984.

In just over a year, I had lost three of the closest people in my life.

After my parents' house sold in November, I moved to Shepherds Croft, one week before Christmas break. Just after we moved, my cat Minnie disappeared as the door had been left open by a workman. Over the next two weeks I called and called for her, and by new year, had reconciled myself to never seeing her again.

One evening I thought I heard a faint "meow". Telling myself I must be hearing things I opened the front door and as I approached my car, this little thin waif that had not eaten in more than two weeks appeared. At least she had not deserted me. Free to come and go through her cat flap entrance door she always came when I called her in from the garden, and lived to be sixteen years old.

Creating the garden, which I changed many elements of over the years, was a therapeutic labour of love after losing three people that had a huge impact on my life at the same time. I remained in this house and made it my own until 2004.

New Opportunities
I responded to an advertisement I had seen in the local paper for a qualified accountant and was interviewed by the managing director and offered the position.

Over a period of 12 years, my expertise as a director and business leader continued to grow. In addition to my professional qualifications in accounting, and the skills I had in systems development and implementation working in a small business, I gained an in-depth understanding of every aspect needed to own and run an SME business. I was also responsible for HR and all aspects of the administration of the company.

In March 2004, the chairman decided to sell the company, which I successfully acquired in a management buyout with 100% of the share capital. The book value of the fixed assets including the building was circa £2 million. The next year, I moved to Hadleigh to be near my business.

Things were going well, and I was enjoying honing my entrepreneurial skills. Then, all of a sudden, life hit me again.

In January 2008 I felt a lump in my left breast. There was no pain and I did not feel unwell. By August, the lump had grown much larger. As a workaholic it was easier to keep focusing on my business and convince myself the lump had been caused by knocking into something, I worked and waited until the middle of September 2008 to book an appointment to see the doctor.

The advice he gave me that day was to leave enough energy to concentrate on the fight for my life rather than my business. As he spoke, telling me that it was 90% certain that the malignant carcinoma required urgent treatment, biopsy at the hospital the next day, and that it was unlikely I would be able to continue to work, it was important for me to remain detached from the words and to remain in control.

I continued to use the 'safe zone story' I had created nine months earlier: "it is benign, a cyst created by knocking into something." Deflecting the sad, disconcerting emotions surrounding the fear of what was to come to the deep recesses of my subconscious, I told myself, this is not happening to me...

The biopsy confirmed the lump was a malignant tumour. Chemotherapy started soon afterwards, followed by radiotherapy and an operation in August 2009. Before I had my operation the doctors indicated I would be in hospital for at least a week. Fortunately, I had a wonderful surgeon who agreed with me that the best place for me to get more rest and recover quicker was home. I was discharged from the hospital within 24 hours of the operation.

The only companion I needed to recover quickly – my beautiful Golden Retriever, Joy – was anxiously waiting at home. Joy intuitively knew she had to be gentle. Her normal unstoppable energy was replaced with complete care and obedience. She hardly left my side, and would instinctively lay asleep beside me, matching her routine with my own. It was weeks before she started pulling on her lead again and chasing rabbits in the field.

I was away from the office for two days when I had my operation and only came in to complete essential work on the remaining days of that week. I am so blessed to have been able to work continuously throughout my treatment.

Meanwhile my company had continued to expand its business activities by becoming a product owner and distributor to the high street retail trade in the months between November of 2007 through to August 2008.

By September, a large number of my distribution and fulfilment clients were lost as a result of the financial crash. The bank had been closely monitoring the company's financial results and restricting the availability of working capital since the beginning of the year. The revenue we needed from the sale of stock to the retail trade did not materialise, paying for the stock that sat in the warehouse had drained the last cash reserves from the bank account, and all of this culminated with a significant proportion of the staff being made redundant on 30th September 2008. The business closed completely in 2012.

Having recovered from cancer I started my accountancy practice, East UK Accountants, and by 2015 I had acquired East UK Accountants (City) Ltd. The business provides the full range of tax and accounting services alongside specialist business consultancy services to individuals, partnerships and companies.

It wasn't long after this that life hit me again.

The second time I had cancer was in 2015 when I had B-Cell lymphoma leading to a series of chemotherapy treatments followed by radiotherapy. At that time I was working from home as my immunity was so low that I needed to be isolated from the risk of any infections, so this was a perfect solution.

Cut to today, my business continues to grow through acquisition and organic growth. This year, I plan to add online membership sites and training courses covering all aspects of starting, growing, owning and running a successful SME business.

Reflecting back over my story, I have faced my personal challenges with fortitude.

God knows everything, including the plan for our lives.

Much as I had tried to save the business, right the way through to September of 2008, it would not have been possible for me to continue to run a £2 million business and 30,000 sq ft building whilst I underwent treatment for cancer. There were less people and responsibilities around me that needed my attention.

My doctor was completely right when he had said saving my own life was more important than the business. I grieved the loss of the business that had been my life and I had fought so hard for. The gift returned to me was that of my own life.

That same determination and the people who truly cared about me brought me through my cancer journey in 2015 stronger than ever before.

Covid-19 has led to a further massive shift in my life, and again it is the people who remain close to me that share that same courage as together we move forward to a better future.

Placing my focus and trust in the source of everything and looking deeply into my inner heart continues to be the only way to find the strength of purpose, power and energy needed to heal my body, mind and spirit. In defining the purpose, passion and dedication with which I have lived and continue to live my life, the words that mean most are those which relate to unconditional love, freely given and received. My personal belief is that God is love, and the source of the love we share with one another. The most important gift that dwells within our spirit. This shapes our 'why', how much we care and who we are.

I am single, independent and determined as ever to face my personal challenges with fortitude continuing to grow and change whilst working towards the ultimate fulfilment of new goals and possibilities in both life and business.

About Me

My education, professional qualifications in business, accountancy and computer technology along with the professional development I undertake are a unique combination. I continuously enhance, update and add to my technical skills and knowledge.

I have written business plans that have secured offers of funding in excess of £1m from two of the major four UK banks in excess of £1m in addition to those from smaller finance houses.

I have acquired multiple accounting and trading businesses of my own as well as assisting my clients to buy and sell their SME enterprises over a period of 20 years.

There are no absolutes in anything. The success we achieve in life and business is determined by the meaningful relationships we nurture and value.

Attending virtual meetings during the long Covid-19 lockdown months provided a precious opportunity to build strong relationships and friendships with experienced partners from across the world.

A challenge provides the opportunity to modify, pivot and change to succeed or even achieve more than we originally planned to.

This chapter is dedicated to two close friends. Michele Risa, a gifted mentor and speaker in life and business. Caring, authentic, dedicated, purposeful and passionate in everything she does. Getting to know Michele for me is a deep reminder of home.

And Bharat Patel, who was there for me throughout my cancer journey in 2015 and has recently retired - a qualified medical doctor who believes in traditional medical science allied to holistic and healing therapies and has been an important part of my life for almost 10 years.

Each of you holds a special place in my heart!

Tanya Grant's Guide To Stand-Out Branding

Tanya Grant
Brand Specialist, Founder & CCI
The TNG Designs Group Limited

"Your brand is a story unfolding across all customer touch points." – Jonah Sachs

Courage, when it comes to the idea of you and your brand, is being able to celebrate the GENIUS of who you are... openly.

You'll be surprised at how many people I come across who actually struggle with this 'simply' because life's lessons and past experiences have told them to feel that they are lesser than what they actually are. It causes them to play small and not take the brave steps of truly getting their brand out there. They feel like no one will take them seriously, they don't want to show off, they are afraid of what feedback they will receive. Is this something that you can relate to?

It's important to know that you are a hell of a lot more than you realise, and your GENIUS is what helps to make you, you. This should be celebrated! And it's something every successful business owner understands.

When you're in touch with your GENIUS, you'll feel empowered in your business, inspired to do everything it takes to help those you serve, and equally, be inspiring to all those who cross your path. Be courageous enough to share

215

your brand and your mission, shout loudly about it, and above all, celebrate it!!! Because if you don't, then why should anybody else?

So what's the first step?

It all starts with understanding why having a 'brand' is important in the first place. Your brand is the one BIG thing that can not only stop you from drowning among the noise of your competition, but what will help you attract the right audience, build better connections and set the right reputation or tone for you, your business and all it entails.

This is what forms the foundation of your GENIUS.

But how do you get there?

Here's a little checklist that'll help you kick-start your brand GENIUS and set it on a more purposeful path to align with who you are today.

Ready?

Great, let's get into it!

#1 Nail Down Your Brand Power Of 3!

Your brand power of three addresses your values, purpose and vision for what it is you do – as well as why you do it. It's what I like to think of as the physiology of a brand. Without it, your brand will fall flat in its communication, making it a confusing journey for both you and your prospective clients. Because, who wants to engage with a brand with no purpose or meaning?

The 'journey' is super important here. Business is not all about your product or service. There's more to being a well-loved brand than that. Your brand 'journey' is how your clients experience you before, during and after the product or service you provide.

When you place importance on refining and defining your values, purpose and vision, along with what your brand journey feels like for your customer, you build that all important know, like and trust factor that is essential to keeping you in business.

What are your brand values?

_____

_____

_____

What is your purpose, your 'why' for what you do?

_____

_____

_____

What is your vision for your brand?

_____

_____

_____

What is your customer's journey before, during and after using your product or service? How do they feel in these three stages?

_____

_____

_____

#2 Pinpoint Your Audience

How many times have you started a conversation with a potential client, only to realise they're not actually serious about making any changes or investing in the value that you provide?

Not only is it a waste of your precious time and energy, but it takes away from people out there who actually need your help and want to make a change.

That's why it's important to ensure that your branding is working for you to attract your ideal audience. That way, you'll have less conversations with people who aren't going to benefit, and more connections with those that need you.

Aside from knowing who they are, the first step is to figure out where your ideal client hangs out. Ask yourself and answer the following questions...

Where does your audience hang out? What communities are they likely to be engaged in?

_____

_____

What are their likes and dislikes? (This can range from anything like spending time with loved ones, supporting charities or causes, all the way through to films, music and entertainment in general)

_____

_____

Once you know where your ideal audience tends to congregate, the next step is to 'value-match' them with what you figured out for your own brand values at checkpoint #1.

When you know their likes and dislikes, you can have more meaningful conversations and help them relate to you.

Commonalities = better conversation = better connection = better chance of people wanting to buy from you.

#3 Become The Figure Of Authority

A brand that is an authority in its field has three crucial elements... belief, certainty and authenticity.

Having these three things is what can help you elevate above the general competition and from those who aren't giving out the added value that you do.

How do you build this? Let me explain...

As a business owner you know the surface level of what your product or service can do for those you serve, right? Well, if you want your brand to rise above the rest, you need to understand and see things a little differently. You need to address the deeper value of what your product or service can truly do for those you serve.

When you build your brand and its products/services in a way that speaks to your clients on a deeper level, you begin to feel more confident in what you stand for and do as a business – because you know you're offering the very best that you can. That's what makes you authentic and what builds your belief system which empowers you to stand out.

And when you can believe in your brand strongly, your certainty increases which, in turn, will help you show up in front of your audience with more confidence and authority.

That being said, it's question time again!

What surface-level direct value do your products/services offer your customers?

_____

_____

What related issues do you feel that your customers may need on a deeper level? How can you support them further and what tools or experience do you have that can help with this?

_____

_____

So there you have it... Your three-point checklist that'll help you build a stand-out brand with courage.

It's exactly what I used when developing my own brand for The TNG Designs Group Limited and it's also what I use to help my clients on their way too.

I recommend going over these points at least twice a year or any time you make a change to what it is that you do. It's always a good idea to make sure that your brand journey still aligns with who you and your business are at that point.

You now have the tools to stay forever courageous as a brand. So go for it! Celebrate your GENIUS.

Here's to your success Queen!

About Me

I am a solution-based brand specialist, multiple international #1 best-selling author, award winning entrepreneur, public speaker and Founder & CCI of multi-disciplined company, The TNG Designs Group Limited. I have collaborated with global brands including the likes of Topshop, Topman, Dorothy Perkins and Miss Selfridge.

Leading with my primary values of Guide, Grounding and Growth, I help business owners stand out from their competition, look and feel like a global brand all so that they can ultimately win new business effortlessly.

It's no easy road when you try to go it alone, especially in business. I know because I tried to for so many years in the past. And don't get me wrong I learnt a hell of a lot along my journey but one MAJOR thing that really stuck with me was to stop trying to go it alone.

It took a while for me to realise that I could let others into my little bubble and get them to help me. Even at that point of acceptance, I needed courage to allow that process to happen, which taught me how to celebrate my GENIUS.

Like you, including so many others, my past experiences have been my life lessons and I use them along with the six key branding principles I discovered, to support my clients and all who come across my path... that includes you!

That's why I'm dedicating this chapter to you and all those who have lost the courage in one way or another. It's time you got out of your own way... borrow a little of my belief in you to help get you going!

Setting Myself Free

Flavia Vilma Leriche-Thompson
Founder
Keep Travel Holidays

"To free yourself from the past you must break the rules of silence and compliance." – Claudia Black

Trigger Warning[1]

I grew up in a small family consisting of two brothers and I. My parents were hard working. Dad worked as a carpenter and farmer, becoming a butcher in the community. He had an entrepreneurial spirit with multiple streams of income. Mum's role was to see to the house and gardening. I had a decent upbringing and never saw poverty.

I looked at my dad over the years trying multiple skills to earn a living so that he could take care of the family. I saw him thriving even in challenging times. I saw the strength of a man that is not willing to stop, no matter the adversity faced.

Being the second child and only daughter, I grew quickly. I started cooking at an early age which became a great hobby, taking care of the house was one of my fantastic chores. I recall my first cooking attempt as a disaster but I was determined to learn. One day my dad gave me two fried fish and I needed to make gravy to go with it. I cooked it and

---

[1] Domestic abuse and suicidal ideation

served my dad, believing it was going to taste good. My dad tasted it and couldn't swallow the gravy. He stood up and desperately reached for the water as I realised it was disastrous.

I was frightened that my dad would be angry and disappointed with me, but he said, "My child, don't be scared. One day you'll get it right." I was surprised by his compassionate response to my bad gravy. From then on I decided and was determined to learn how to cook and continued with my dad's encouragement to measure and weigh my ingredients. Sure enough, my food became better and better each day.

Womanhood

As I grew into a young woman, I found it hard to come to terms with who I was becoming.

My mother was a strict woman, who wouldn't allow me to even sleep over with friends so I learned to play alone, talk alone and be alone. I asked myself once, "Is that right?" My friends are sleeping over with other friends and my best friend comes to sleep over at my home but I was never allowed to sleep over. I had a lot of unanswered questions.

Once, she said to me, "If you ever talk to a boy, you will get pregnant!" So anytime a boy would come close to me I would run for my life! Run, pregnancy is coming! I was so confused and couldn't understand why I would get pregnant just from talking to a boy. I had no knowledge and understanding about conception.

The years went by and thankfully, I was sent to a girls school where I was happy and safe from boys that could get me pregnant just by talking to them…

My mother was on top of the world that I passed the entrance exam and that it was a no-boys school. I also saw it as a great accomplishment. It was a ray of light and flying colours with butterflies in my belly.

I adapted to the all-girls school really well and I joined the choir. I love singing, and my dad always encouraged me with my hobbies. My mum was not interested though. My dad always complimented me and always wanted to listen to me. Our father-daughter relationship was great.

One day I wanted to go to a festival which I had my dad's approval for but my mum opposed. She was always opposing and it made my relationship with her difficult. My dad would be quiet as my mother screamed the house down. I often kept myself to myself and began to question whether my mum really loves me.

I desperately wanted answers so I went to an older lady with my questions. I asked her, "Why doesn't my mum love me?" She looked at me with a smile and said, "Little girl, ask God so you can have love for your mum and ask God for your mum to have love for you." I was surprised at her answer.

We prayed then, and I had tears in my eyes. She patted my back and told me that everything's going to be alright. I was confused and didn't understand what went on but I felt peace.

I got home and immediately started my chores before my mum returned from the market. Dinner was cooked, laundry was washed, floors were swept and mopped.

As soon as my mum entered she asked, "Have you done all your chores?"

"Yes mother," I answered.

"Did you do the ceiling?" I said no. She started screaming the house down and I became upset thinking that nothing I did was enough.

My dad heard me running, crying. He had a big box and asked me to get in, covering me as my mum arrived and asked "Where is she?"

My dad pretended not to know and I waited safely in the box. He had saved me from receiving another beating.

Things were not so good outside of the home either. Walking home from school, I experienced a bully who called me names. She had an adopted sister who joined in and the two of them bullied me relentlessly. I told my mum about it, she said nothing, she did nothing. It carried on for a year.

I tried to be brave but I cried every night. I wet the bed every night. I was frightened and scared. I began hating school and I resented my mum.

After years of bullying, I decided to take matters into my own hands. I hated myself so much and I wanted to take my last breath. I decided to drink my dad's poison (grass killer) but it was so smelly that I couldn't go ahead. I pondered a while saying to myself there must be another way.

At the age of sixteen, a young man called Jack had befriended me. One Saturday, I was taking care of my younger brother and I took him and my friend out with me. Little did I know that the neighbours would tell my mum. The news scattered like wildfire. My mother called me and later started screaming the house down and I got my beating. I felt hopeless, defeated and terrible.

I ran to my grandmother who lived two miles down the road. She received me, nursed me and I stayed with her over-night. My cousin popped round and said if my mother catches me she will beat me more. When I heard that I knew what I had to do.

The next day, Jack came to see me in the middle of the night. I told him I had to go with him or else they will kill me. I had done all my thinking and had nothing to lose. No more beating, no more abuse, no more calling names. I wanted to put all that behind me. I just needed a saviour and I was looking for somebody to say they love me, appreciate me, value me and accept me. At midnight we left my grandmother's house for safety. I didn't know where he was taking me, I just needed somebody to safeguard me. I reflected as we were travelling. I felt a joy that I couldn't express.

I told Jack about everything I had been through and he told me he loved me. I moved in with him and his mother and as the months went on, we fell deeper in love.

Pain And Joy

In July 1985 I became pregnant and I couldn't get my head around it. It happened so suddenly and I remembered what mother had told me about talking to boys. Nobody prepared me for pregnancy. My mother hadn't taught me and we weren't educated on it at school. I didn't know how to protect myself. I felt the world should swallow me up. I was still only sixteen years old.

I felt so naïve and stupid. I didn't resist anything because I was searching for love in the wrong place.

Sadly Jack started to change for the worse. He started going out every day, leaving me alone at his mum's house. He came home at midnight on many occasions.

One day, I was feeling quite unwell from the pregnancy so I cooked his dinner early and left it on the table. He came in and moaned about it being cold. I was in bed when he came in, pulling me off in anger. I cried, this couldn't be happening to me again, facing aggression from the one who said he would love me and not hit me.

I couldn't understand why I had to go through hardship in life. I asked myself, why am I not a desirable woman? Why am I not a lovable woman?

By the time my due date drew nearer, Jack had changed completely. As I counted the days to becoming a young mother, I was just empty, hopeless, and clueless of what to do.

In April 1986, I gave birth to my first daughter, weighing 5lbs 8oz, healthy with plenty of hair looking exactly like him. I was so excited that the delivery went well and the baby was okay.

The day I was discharged from hospital, I arrived home to Jack who was horrible and wanted me to cook for him immediately. I was poorly, still in pain and could not stand for long. It was only then that I realised love had gone out of the window but I was so young with nowhere else to go.

As a young mother, I did my best and had to learn everything by myself. I became a grown woman even though I was a teenager. I continued to do the best I could and it brings joy to my heart that my daughter grew up healthy.

Gazing at her and reflecting on all the adversity I had gone through, I wished that she would never have to experience anything like it.

Stand Up For What's Right

Two years later, I fell pregnant again and gave birth to my second daughter in April 1988. She was healthy and well at 6lbs 5oz and was a bouncy baby girl who filled me with joy and gladness. I was so pleased to give my eldest daughter a sister because I never had one myself. I was sure that they would be there for each other and love each other unconditionally.

The day went by and Jack's relatives came by to visit. Here it goes again, Jack wants me to cook. He refuses to go to the kitchen not even to warm water far less to cook. I thought for myself that I cannot continue this way. It is abusive if a man sees his partner is in pain and forces her to cook. I drew a line underneath it and promised myself that I need to be out of this relationship.

Jack remained abusive, and with two young children I knew I couldn't spend the rest of my life with him. I certainly couldn't have a third child with him.

I started to question what if he was helpful and supportive? What if he was not a woman abuser and a bully? What if he had chosen to treat me better? What if he had managed his anger? What if he chose not to lay a finger on me? What if he chose not to say, I will kill you? I decided to put a stop to the beating, the hitting, the abusing, the bullying.

This time I promised myself to be on alert, to look after myself and let no man destroy my worth.

I wanted to pick up my education where I left off as a high school drop-out so I could be the best mother for my two children. In the middle of the night, I woke up from my sleep and decided to leave. My children were young and vulnerable, and I didn't want to stay a minute longer under the same roof as an abuser and bully.

It was really difficult. I thought about the kids growing up without their dad. It was a tough decision but it was the best for them and for me; as the broken, hopeless, sad, weak, empty, wrecked and scared woman that I was.

It was the best decision I ever made for my children and I.

By taking that big step, I at once became more courageous, resistant, resilient, fearless, brave and confident. I had to be all of the above in order to stand up to a bully and all the abuse that I suffered in our relationship.

Jack had always promised me he would change but he never did. He couldn't manage his anger and would not be able to bring our children up in the right way. I had to stand up for all that is right and set myself free as a woman of destiny.

About Me

I am the Founder of Keep Travel Holidays, bringing people joy, relaxation and unforgettable experiences.

In my other business, Yummy Pot and Sauces, I work as a chef and have catered for Barbados High Commission functions since 2004. I am very passionate about cooking and feeding others. Cooking is fun and joyful for me and I forever get ideas for new menus coming to my mind.

I also place great value in sharing stories with people. I would like to inspire people with my story and in doing so, positively impact their lives to help them have better relationships and make better choices in their lives.

Conclusion

We hope that whilst reading this collection of powerful stories, it has encouraged you to reflect on your own journey and times you have had to find courage of your own. There are many lessons we can learn here, as these stories take us to places both familiar as well as those never imagined. Life, as we know, is never a straight road, but with determination, strength and resilience there are many situations we can overcome. Sometimes we just have to face life's challenges head on.

There are many common themes that can help as well as guide us.

- Take time for reflection. Getting clear on who you are, why you're here and aligning to your purpose
- Heal wounds of the past to enable you to flourish both in your present and your future
- Believe in yourself
- Listen to your intuition
- Embrace change
- Invest in yourself as it's your journey to growth
- Work on your mindset
- Challenge the status quo and don't be afraid to go against the grain
- Stand up for your values and beliefs

The obstacles we face are often not of our own choosing, but on reflection we may be surprised just how far we've come. We should appreciate and celebrate those qualities that have allowed us to grow and keep moving forward.

To find strength in the midst of challenge, pain and grief is not always easy, but we CAN do it.

When we find our voice, we find our courage and then we emerge as wiser, stronger and more empowered Queens.

About Queens In Business

Our Why

Today female entrepreneurs are making waves in the world. There have never been more of us rising up, standing up for what we believe in and building our own vehicle for freedom.

It's our belief that each and every female entrepreneur has what it takes to be successful. Everyone has a gift inside of them, a skill or knowledge that could help someone who is struggling right now.

Female entrepreneurs have the ability to contribute to the world and deserve the opportunity to be successful, feel fulfilled and be visible within their business.

The journey of entrepreneurship can be challenging at times and with just a fraction of women taking the leap to start their own businesses it can be a lonely ride.

That's why we created the Queens In Business Club.

The Queens In Business Club is more than just a community. It's a movement created to recognise the achievements of female entrepreneurs, to support and guide them and give them the tools to increase their exposure in business.

Co-founded by five of us, it's the first of its kind, created by female entrepreneurs for female entrepreneurs:

Chloë Bisson – The Automation Queen

Carrie Griffiths – The Speaking Queen

Shim Ravalia – The Health Queen

Sunna Coleman – The Writing Queen

Tanya Grant – The Branding Queen

Before starting the QIB Club, we'd all built our own successful businesses, spent huge amounts of money on training and mentorship and invested years in growing our businesses.

We learned and mastered specific strategies and methods to get our businesses where they are today and we are now sharing those learnings and experiences with the members of the QIB Club.

Whether it is having a successful business or becoming financially independent, we aim to provide female entrepreneurs with the tools they need and a community to support them along the way.

Our Methodology

We believe that in business the ability to achieve success comes down to three core pillars:

- Education
- Empowerment
- Execution

Education for us means having the right skills, knowledge and strategies to achieve your goals and if you don't have them right now, having access to learn from experts that do.

Empowerment is about surrounding yourself with the right people to support you and cheer for you on the journey. It is about creating an empowering environment that nourishes you to be the best that you can be.

Execution means having the motivation, determination and drive to do what it takes to get to your end goal. Where we may struggle to find the motivation within ourselves, it's about having mentors to encourage you and giving you a kick up the bum when you need it.

At Queens In Business, we've created a powerful methodology that combines all three of the core pillars.

We provide the hands-on business education from world class experts with the push you need to execute your strategies whilst surrounding you with supportive members to empower you to overcome any roadblocks that come up on the way.

Our Mission
We're on a mission to change the world of entrepreneurship.

We want to create a movement that empowers female entrepreneurs and encourages their drive for success, not belittles it or judges them for putting their career first.

We want to eliminate the fear of judgement and the fear of failure. We want to create a world where it's okay to ask for help, it's okay to express your challenges and it's okay to make mistakes.

We want to support female entrepreneurs in becoming powerful role models for future generations who will believe in their abilities and believe they can achieve what they want.

It's our mission to provide support and exposure to Queens all over the world regardless of their age, background, or their position in their business.

It's time now for female entrepreneurs to rise up and be leaders, fight for what they want for themselves and for others, and to come out the other side, stronger than ever.

To find out more about the Queens In Business Club, go to:
www.queensinbusinessclub.com

Contact us on:
team@queensinbusinessclub.com

Printed in Great Britain
by Amazon